THE DAY IS SO
LONG AND THE
WAGES SO SMALL

ALSO BY SAMUEL CHARTERS

Poetry
The Children
The Landscape At Bolinas
Heroes Of The Prize Ring
Days
To This Place
From A London Notebook
From A Swedish Notebook
Of Those who Died

Fiction
Mr Jabi And Mr Smythe
Jelly Roll Morton's Last Night At The Jungle Inn
Louisiana Black
Elvis Presley Talks To His Mother After The Ed Sullivan Show

Criticism
Some Poems/Poets: Studies in American Underground Poetry Since 1945

Biography
I Love: The Story of Vladimir Mayakovsky And Lili Brik
(with Ann Charters)

Memoir
A Country Year

Translations
Baltics (from the Swedish of Tomas Tranströmer)
We Women (from the Swedish of Edith Södergran)
The Courtyard (from the Swedish of Bo Carpelan)

Anthologies
Literature And Its Writers (with Ann Charters)

Music
Jazz: New Orleans 1885–1957
The Country Blues
Jazz: A History Of The New York Scene
The Poetry Of The Blues
The Bluesmen
Robert Johnson
The Legacy Of The Blues
Sweet As The Showers Of Rain
Spelmännen (The Swedish Fiddlers)
The Roots Of The Blues
The Bluesmakers

THE DAY IS SO LONG AND THE WAGES SO SMALL

MUSIC ON A SUMMER ISLAND

SAMUEL CHARTERS

MARION BOYARS
NEW YORK • LONDON

Published in the United States and Great Britain
in 1999 by Marion Boyars Publishers
237 East 39th Street, New York NY 10016
24 Lacy Road, London SW15 1NL
Distributed in Australia and New Zealand by
Peribo Pty Ltd, 58 Beaumont Road, Mount Kuring-gai, NSW

British Library Cataloguing in Publication Data
Charters, Samuel
     The day is so long and the wages so small: music on a
     summer island
     1. Charters, Samuel—Biography   2. Authors, American—
     20th century—Biography   3. Sound—Recording and
     reproducing—Bahamas—Andros Island   4. Andros Island
     (Bahamas)—Social life and customs   I. Title
     813.5'4
Library of Congress Cataloging-in-Publication-Data
Charters, Samuel Barclay.
     The day is so long and the wages so small: music on a
     summer island / Samuel Charters.
          p.   cm.
     ISBN 0–7145–3056–5 (pbk. : alk. paper)
     1. Folk music—Bahamas—History and criticism.
     2. Charters, Samuel Barclay—Journeys—Bahamas.
     3. Bahamas—Description and travel.   I. Title.
ML3565.C53   1999
781.62'9697296--dc21   98–46735
                                                  CIP
                                                  MN
ISBN 0-7145-3056-5 Paperback
The right of Samuel Charters to be identified as author of this work has been
asserted by him in accordance with the Copyright, Designs and Patents Act 1998
Typeset in 12/13½ pt Garamond by
Ann Buchan (Typesetters), Shepperton
Printed in Great Britain by
Redwood Books, Trowbridge, Wiltshire

Now the day is so long and the wages so small,
    Long summer day,
The day is so long and the wages so small,
    She's a long summer day . . .

             Frederick McQueen

CONTENTS

LIST OF ILLUSTRATIONS

AN INTRODUCTORY NOTE

Some of you reading this book may be a little uncomfortable with quotations from conversations I describe that happened more than forty years ago. Is this what people really said to him? Does he really remember all that? I don't know anyone who can remember with any accuracy most of the things that were said to them forty years ago. I can't remember everything either, but like everyone else who does any extensive field recording, I took notes at the time I was with the people I was recording, and the notes are the source of the conversations. I once wrote in an article that one of the things that's best about working in the field is that you can always say where you were on a certain day. I can say with certainty that on August 2, 1958, I was dancing to a small 'jump up' band beside on open fire on the beach at Fresh Creek Settlement on Andros Island in the Bahamas and I can say, just as certainly, what people said to each other at the boat landing later that night as the music and the dancing wound down.

All of the music described in the book was released on four long-playing records by Folkways Records in New York City in 1959 and in the early 1960s. I have freely adapted and expanded the notes that I wrote for the albums when they were first released. Someone who is familiar with the albums might have noticed the name A.R. Danberg listed as photographer and technical assistant. A.R. Danberg was Ann Ruth Danberg, who was twenty-one, a graduate of the University of California at Berkeley the year before, and who was going on in the fall of 1958 to study for a master's degree at Columbia. Because of our personal and family situations we felt it was necessary to be careful about using her name. In the notes to the recordings and in the descriptions of the life on the island that summer I often used the pronoun 'I,' when it should have been 'we'. We were married in the spring of 1959, and she became Ann Charters. Her own long and distinguished career as a writer, biographer, anthologist, literary scholar, photographer and occasional pianist had some of its beginnings in the little wood frame house we shared at the edge of a tidal creek on Andros that summer so long ago.

Samuel Charters
Stockholm, 1998

1

A Different Kind Of Music

From the swaying deck of a small boat, standing off the
barrier reef in the summer of 1958, the coast line of Andros
Island, the largest of the Out Islands of the Bahamas, was a
ragged, littered shore of deserted beaches and low headlands.
The prevailing winds swept off the shore, and the sea surged
across the reef to the warm shallows off the beach. The
occasional sails of native fishing boats danced uncertainly in
the haze of the afternoon sun. Boats drew close to pass, and
voices called across the water. The island was quiet, except for
the cries of small birds hidden in the leaves of the trees.
Bunched along the skyline there were the spindly trunks and
the fringed hanging crowns of palm trees. Small settlements,
usually a day's sail apart, were scattered along the shore. A
settlement was a few houses in the trees behind the beach,
with the boats pulled up into a shallow creek or anchored in
the deeper water off shore. Women in faded dresses hunted
along the beach for shells, and children played at the edge of
the water. From the scattered houses narrow paths, scraped
into the gray-brown stone, led through the coarse brush to
smaller settlements a mile or so behind the shore. The outlines of small wooden frame houses or weather-beaten stucco
buildings could be seen through the low ridges.

It was a poor island, except for the few weeks in the early
winter when the boats came in from the crawfish beds with
the money from the season's catch. There were small farms

back in the brush, but a few plantings exhausted the thin soil covering the crumbling stone and sand. There were a few pigs, some chickens, and small herds of goats, but fish was the most important food, cooked with rice brought from Nassau on the fishing boats. The interior of the island was deserted, covered with shallow lakes or pine barrens, with mosquitoes and flies filling the air. Andros had been dogged with such endless bad fortune that many of the older natives felt the island was haunted.

In that summer of 1958, except for a handful of white residents in two or three of the larger settlements, the eight or nine hundred people scattered along the Andros coast were black, the descendants of Bahamian slaves. One of the cruelties of slavery that is often forgotten is that slavery scattered people. It left them flung across the earth in places they didn't know, and that in the beginning they couldn't leave. They were thrown together in odd handfuls — people who didn't have enough language in common to speak to each other in anything but the slaver's language, and who had lost the open vestiges of their culture, however much still was hidden away to be found there in the future. They were thrown into places like Jamaica, where the sugar plantations killed more than were born, or they were strewn over places like Alabama and Mississippi, where it was possible to put together some kind of a life, if they could struggle free of the slavers' control. They were also flung onto places like Andros. When nothing seemed to work on the Out Islands of the Bahamas for the few slave owners who arrived there, they left their slaves behind them to survive the best they could. The struggle was still going on for the people of Andros.

How had I come to Andros in 1958? How had I even known about an island that was almost forgotten and off any kind of traveler's route? It was music that took me there. A different kind of music from anything I had ever heard before. It is hard now to remember back to that moment and think of how little we knew about the music of the world's many countries, societies, and cultures in the beginning of the 1950s. People like me who were excited by music of every kind had a sort of map in our minds, a map that was made up of sounds and rhythms, songs and dances, instead of the usual lines of rivers and boundaries and coastlines. In those years our map of the world's music still looked like the maps of the world's continents from two or three hundred years before. There were whole empty spaces where we couldn't tell you what the music might sound like, what instruments the musicians played, what songs they sang. On some of the early navigators' maps the empty areas at the edge of the known world were filled in with decorative drawings of nymphs playing on trumpets made of conch shells. For all we knew that's what the music there sounded like.

But Andros?

I wouldn't have known about the music of Andros if it had not been for the earlier recordings that had been done of Andros musicians by Alan Lomax. Lomax had begun recording African-American music in the early 1930s, when he was a teenager. Working first with his father, John A. Lomax, and then for the American Library of Congress, he recorded and documented every style of music everywhere he found it. In the late 1930s he came to the Bahamas. In 1958 we met people who still remembered him from his trip there. They remembered sailing with him on a native sloop, and when it got too hot on the open deck, Alan dove into the sea and swam underneath the boat, splashing to the surface on the other side.

The Library of Congress, when it had a little money, pressed small quantities of 78 rpm singles of some of the music that its field collectors were gathering. Although we all knew about Muddy Waters and his Chicago blues band, on a Library of Congress single we had already heard Muddy when he was still a field hand named McKinley Morganfield on the Stovall Plantation in Mississippi, when Alan had recorded him in 1940. The singles were hard to get. They weren't sold in stores. You had to send for them, and for most of us who were interested in the music it was too complicated to find the order forms and the record lists, and to decide what address to use for the package that would finally show up in the mail.

I first heard one of the singles that the Library of Congress released of Alan's Andros recordings in Berkeley in the winter of 1955. A few months before, I had left New Orleans, where I had been gathering material for a book about the city's African-American musicians, and I was a student at the University of California, trying to get some kind of degree so I could finally make a living doing something more practical than traveling through the South with a tape recorder. I was taking Economics courses, but I was also crowding in as many music courses as I could. In the mornings I would bicycle down early from the top of the Berkeley hills, where I was living in a weathered redwood cottage almost engulfed by low-limbed trees and an overgrown garden, so I could spend an hour in the music library. Along with most of the musicians I knew, and all of my friends, I was listening to everything. We sat up late at night in our cramped, damp cottages, drinking cheap wine and playing whatever we had just found for each other. It was during that winter that I almost memorized Stravinsky's opera *The Rake's Progress*, I wrote a long paper on the use of tonality in the music of Charles Ives, I listened to classical music from Japan and Indonesia, I was working on a special project in seventeenth-century English opera, I was hanging out in Mexican restaurants in Oakland to listen to mariachi bands, and I had begun the book about the New Orleans musicians I had been interviewing and recording.

And I was listening to the music of Andros.

The Andros single was one of several Library of Congress records that the music library had ordered. I don't think anyone had noticed particularly what they were. There were Kentucky mountain ballads, five-string banjo playing, McKinley Morganfield's blues, field hollers, and play party songs. What was so startling about the Andros music was that it was so different from everything else. All African-American music is a tangle of influences and conflicting traditions, which finally coalesce into new musical idioms that take something from all of their cultural backgrounds. The song that I couldn't get out of my head didn't even take one side of a 10 inch 78 single. It was called 'Dig My Grave'.

Alan had recorded it sung on the dock with a group of men who had sailed into Nassau from Andros on one of their fishing boats. The song sounded like an eighteenth-century anthem, and the men sang it as a kind of polyphonic round. I had never heard the African musical idiom transposed onto music from that early period. It was beautifully sung, and there was a sensitive shaping between the men's voices. Were there more songs like it? Was it even possible, almost twenty years later, to find men like the group who had recorded it then?

I bicycled down the hill early all the spring of 1955, and I listened to 'Dig My Grave' so often that I could hear every part of the counterpoint in my head. I was so involved in other music of that style — English polyphony — that the Andros singing took on a even stronger resonance for me. I would get there sometime. I just had no idea when.

It was three years later before I could think of Andros again. In 1958 I was living in New York, and Ann Danberg, whom I had met in music classes in Berkeley, drove to New York late in the spring and we found a cheap room in a crumbling building on East Sixteenth Street. She had been awarded a

Woodrow Wilson Fellowship to begin studying for a master's degree at Columbia University in September, but she had the summer free. Just as important, she had a small car, the green Chevrolet coupé she had driven from California and we both had saved a little money from jobs we had worked over the winter. Could we go to Andros? She had heard the little Andros song and she was as intrigued about the music as I was. We had to decide so many things, and we had so much to work out between us. Why not travel to Andros, and take the summer to see what our life together might be like? When I think back to that summer it isn't only the music and the people that I remember. It is the innocence of the summer that is still such a strong memory. We were young enough to think anything could be possible, and for those long months of the summer on the island, almost everything was.

We didn't, of course, know how to get to Andros. Part of our innocence that summer was our hopeless ignorance of what we were doing. What saved the uncertainties of the traveling for us was that it didn't matter to us how things would work out. We just believed that somehow they all would. We looked at a map and saw that Andros was close to Florida. It looked like it wasn't far from Miami. The way to begin, then, was to drive to Miami. We had never traveled together, but we knew we couldn't take much with us, so there wasn't much to argue about. Ann had to take some books for a language exam that she faced in the fall, and by the time I had filled a traveling bag with all the things I needed for the tape recorder — the plugs and connections and extension cords — tapes and microphones — I had very little room for clothes, but it didn't matter because I didn't have many clothes. Ann had just as little, since when she left California she wasn't sure what was going to happen when she came to New York. We stuffed any other books we had into the spaces left in our bags. The only place either of us had to live was the roach-infested room in New York, and there was no difficulty leaving everything in the room behind. I had a tape recorder — a bulky Pentron machine that had already been with me through some of the southern states, California, and Mexico — and we packed it in the trunk of Ann's coupé, piled the rest of our bags around it and drove through the Holland Tunnel to begin the long, steamy, summer drive to Florida.

2

An Island The Wrong Side
Of The Wind

When we looked at a map of the Bahamas it seemed obvious that Andros Island would be the first place we'd reach after we left the Florida coast, but for us nothing about Andros was as simple as the map suggested, even if it is the largest of all the islands that make up the Bahamas and it is only 150 miles east of the Florida coast. Some of the other island nations of the Caribbean, like Barbados, are much smaller. Andros is 120 miles long and 45 miles wide, but what the maps don't show is that most of Andros is a mosquito-infested swamp. The west coast, the coast that faces Miami, is a long, hot, shallow mud flat. The water is rich with fish and submerged plant life, but the ocean, even at high tide, is less than four feet deep. There's no break in the mud for a harbor. Along the east coast, the side of the island that faces the Bahamas capitol of Nassau on the small island of New Providence, there is a shallow, dangerous reef. Any kind of vessel drawing more than four or five feet of water must anchor outside the reef, and rely on cables to keep from dragging with the wind.

To complicate the map of Andros, the island is divided by wide sluggish streams called 'bights', that separate it below its waist into two parts. The bights are too shallow and too tangled for a boat to cross the island, but they are broad enough that the natives have to sail their clumsy boats across

BERRY
ISLANDS

Little Harbour
Cay

Bonds Cay

Northeast Providence Channel

Whale Cay

Frazers Hog
Cay

Joulters Cays

Nicholls Town

Booby
Cay

Paradise
Island

Cable
Beach

Rose
Island

Gambier

NASSAU

Clifton

New
Providence

Yellow
Bank

Williams
Island

Fresh Creek

Andros
Island

Cargill Creek

Big Wood
Cay

Tongue of the Ocean

Bight

Lisbon Creek

Mangrove
Cay

Griggs Hill

Yellow
Cay

Middle

Green
Cay

Kemps Bay

Congo Town

High Point
Cay

Mars Bay

Well
Cay

Water
Cays

Curly Cut
Cays

rricane

Flats

the surging currents to travel from one part of the island to the other.

When I tried to learn more about Andros, months later, I found very little in the libraries about it. Pirates used some of its coves sporadically in the eighteenth century to raid on the shipping using the channel between Andros and the main Bahamian islands. Two hundred years later there had been a flurry of smuggling, with large speed boats that ran alcohol into Florida during the American prohibition, but other islands in the Bahamas group were more accessible to the Florida coast, and they had better harbors. There had been some attempts at commercial enterprises on the island — a pineapple farm and a lumber mill — but nothing had survived. For the people who lived on Andros, scattered in their small settlements along the east coast, the physical reality that had forced them into isolation was something they were helpless to change. The prevailing winds blow from west to east, and it is an arduous sail back from Nassau to one of the villages. For fishermen in small, clumsy, hand built sloops, depending on ragged sails, the winds were the reality that shaped their lives. Andros is an island on the wrong side of the wind.

We didn't know any of this when we walked the streets of Miami, trying to find some way to cross the 150 miles of Gulf Stream to the island. We walked from shipping office to shipping office, asking if anyone knew of any kind of ship going to Andros. Miami was the same as it is every summer. As another writer described it, the streets were like a furnace and the sun was an executioner. The city was hot. It was hot and damp and airless and sticky and our clothes clung to us in sagging folds.

We were already running out of fresh clothes. Since we had so little money we'd spent some sticky nights sleeping in the car, and we were wrinkled and sweaty and insect bitten. We also seemed to be the only ones who were outside walking in the sun. No one left their downtown office buildings except for a sudden rush at lunch-time, when they streamed past us in a struggle to get from their air-conditioned office to an air-conditioned restaurant with as little time on the street as possible. If they had to go anywhere else in the city they drove there. When we walked into one of the shipping offices or into a travel bureau and stopped in the chill air the office workers in their cool dresses and light jackets looked up at our sweating faces and clinging shirts with surprised sympathy. In our anxious efforts to save money we had begun cutting each other's hair, and neither of us was very skilled at it. I remember that most of the women wore their hair in elaborate beehives that must have taken hours to set. It was the style then in the South, and their hair was set so carefully that it kept its waves and swirls and climbing ringlets through the whole day at the office. Ann's short trimmed, perfunctorily brushed hair was as out of place as our faded shirts and tennis shoes.

We quickly learned that there were dozens of ways to get to Nassau, but there wasn't much of any way to get anywhere else in the islands, unless we could hire a plane to take us, and with a glance the agents knew immediately that we weren't going to hire a plane. There was a cheap way to get there, but it was the least interesting; a ticket on a Miami-Nassau cruise ship.

'I just know you can get anywhere you want from Nassau,' persuaded a woman with relentlessly fluffed hair and a tired smile in the ticket office of the cruise ship line. We went outside and spent another hour on the stifling streets, trying to find some other way to get across to the island. We did all the things travelers do when they have to make a decision, which meant counting our money and looking at the map again. We might finally find a cheaper way, but it could take us so long that we'd spend as much of our meager funds waiting in Miami. The cruise ship it would have to be. We

went back to the woman with the tired smile. She had space
on a cruise ship that was sailing the next afternoon.

We had found a place to stay in a run-down rooming house
south of the main part of the city, and the woman owning it
wiped her face with a towel, smiled and suggested that for
$20 she'd let us park Ann's car under a tree in her backyard.
In our innocence — in that summer of 1958 — it seemed
possible that the car would still be there when we got back
from Andros. We spent a last night in the rooming house's
musty bed, then the next morning we drove the car into the
shade under the tree, picked up our suitcases and the tape
recorder and went off to the Miami-Nassau Pleasure Cruise.

The folder we were handed with our cruise ship tickets announ-
ced that we would enjoy 'Dancing, moonlit nights on the
romantic upper deck, night club entertainment, greetings in
Nassau harbor from smiling boys who will dive for pennies
. . .' All of this had nothing to with the kind of experience
we had come to the Bahamas to find, but we seemed to be the
only people who were disappointed, since everyone else obviously was completely satisfied with a floating version of their
local motel. What we found when we finally got to Nassau
was that the hotels where our fellow passengers were going to
stay were just like the ship, and it would have been easier for
everyone if Nassau could have been towed across the Gulf
Stream and anchored off Miami Beach, so that people could
avoid the inconvenience of having to get there.

How different were the expectations of all of us who crowded
onto the ship and were more or less presented to each other.
The formal dinner was as awkward for us, in our wash shirts
and wrinkled pants, as it was for the other couples who had
been put at the table with us. The men were wearing suits or
jackets, with white shirts, striped ties, and golf course tans.
The women were in elaborate dinner dresses, with gathers,

folds, and pleats. Since all of the women in the dining room were wearing the same kind of dress it must have been the style that year in southern Florida. Like almost every other Florida woman we'd seen their hair was set in busy weaves of waves and curls, as if there were going to be a contest later in the evening for the best preserved hairstyle. They were all southerners, and our northern accents, when we did say something, made them even more uneasy. There was a tacit understanding that it would be a little awkward to include us in their conversation; so they carefully looked away and talked with each other.

But I have to be fair, and I'm sure they must have been as disappointed with us as we were with them. They hadn't paid for a moonlight cruise and put on their party clothes to sit at a table with two people who looked as if they should be cleaning the cabins. What did they see when they occasionally glanced over at us in the wavering light of the ship's candles? I have to look at photographs from that summer to remember what we each looked like — since a face you've seen change over the years is only a blur when you try to remember any particular moment. In the photographs we mostly looked very young, and we stared at everything with a little more intensity than was really necessary. In our cotton shirts and faded pants, everything needing to be ironed, we looked even poorer than we were. My hair was cut short and my face mostly looked thin and angular. I was taller than the other people at the table, but I was also thinner. Some of the other men at the table had short hair, but Ann was the only woman whose hair wasn't set. It was not only short and black, it was also naturally curly. She was easy to travel with because she never had to do anything about it. A moment with a hair brush in the morning, usually while she talked about something else over her shoulder, was good enough, and she was ready to set off. She wasn't as tall as I was, and she didn't have the same square shoulders, but she was even younger and just as slim, and she looked very beautiful, covertly glancing around at the rest of the table with intent blue eyes under her startling black eyebrows.

The 'night club entertainment' was a gray-haired purser who sang and did a little soft shoe number, and as soon as he was finished we left the others at the table to the dance floor and fled up to the 'romantic upper deck'. No matter what else is superficial and depressing about a cruise ship there is no way to completely dispel the atmosphere of an open deck in the moonlight. The deck was broad and dark and, except for a myriad of deck chairs it was empty, just as it had been advertised. The moon was rising through a light mist ahead of us, and behind the ship a long sweeping trail of phosphorus glistened delicately in the moonlight. We were still sitting in the darkness on a pair of deck chairs we'd pulled close together when the ship passed the first of the small outer islands of the Bahamas chain, threading through them on its plodding way to Nassau. Somewhere to the south of us was the dark shape of Andros, invisible above the streaked, shadow lines of the waves.

Though I think of this summer of 1958 as a moment when we both were so innocent, I know nothing could ever have been as innocent as our angry feelings when we woke up and realized that we weren't moving any longer, and we went up on the deck and saw shining, wet, black-skinned boys diving into the clear water of the harbor for pennies. It was obvious to us that they didn't much like diving for pennies, despite their fixed, grinning smiles. If there had been any other way to get pennies they wouldn't have gotten up so early to stand in their battered wooden boats, waiting for someone to throw something so they could fight with each other over the fading coins as they fluttered their way down into the water. But when we walked to the other side of the deck we could see fishermen in the distance, solitary black men in tiny hand-made boats who watched the tumult around the clumsy cruise ship as it were part of another world. They were from the Bahamas we had come to find.

In 1958 it was also possible to get away from the oppressive artifice of Nassau's main street, Bay Street, which ran along the waterfront. The 'native market' — with its grimacing black women in shapeless print dresses holding out battered hats — was close to the landing for the cruise ships, but if you walked a few hundred yards away from the harbor you left most of it behind you. Along the water the tourist hotels looked like they had been constructed from the same set of architect's drawings that had been used for the hotels in Miami, but off Bay Street, on the slight rise as the streets led inland, there were buildings that still looked as if they'd been built by someone who had been born on the island and knew what its weather was like and knew something about the island's old way of life.

All the incongruities of tourism — in that summer so long ago — still were only a thin veneer pressed over a society that persisted in its own habits and attitudes. It was a society that still hadn't decided if it wanted to turn every-thing into Bay Street. Beyond the end of the tourist strip we could see older, well built houses with the feeling of an English seaside town. There was an Anglican chapel, and there were rows of trimmed bushes and carefully tended trees close to the side walk. Every house had an English garden, with a flush of bright flowers. There was still a city with its own character and way of life.

We had no idea where we could stay, but we were certain that if we just kept walking away from the water we'd find something that would suit us. We turned away from Bay Street and kept on walking up the low hills, heaving up our bags with arms that had begun to protest against the heat and the weight. It wasn't our bags I was struggling with. We only

had the few clothes we'd taken out of the trunk of Ann's car.
Shirts and wash pants, bathing suits and shorts. Ann had her
German text books for her language exam, and there were the
few books we'd found room for in the bags. What was weighing me down as I strained to make it from one stretch of shade
to the next was the dead weight of the tape recorder. It was as
large as a suitcase and three times as heavy, and the other
suitcase I was carrying was stuffed full of the things that I
needed to make the recorder work. There were the cords,
reels, tapes, microphones (I had two in case one was damaged)
and a variety of plugs, cables, and jacks. In 1958, you had to
have this much equipment with you if you wanted to do any
recording. There were no easily portable recording machines,
and the world still was getting along as best it could without
cassette players.

But then in 1958 you didn't have to walk so far. The rising
streets led away from the waterfront and its tourist crowds,
and when the street sloped down again we found ourselves in
a neighborhood of small, narrow dirt streets, plastered walls,
and weathered board houses, the windows left open and the
curtains dangling out over the sills. The faces turning to look
at us were black and, instead of advertisements the walls were
hung with thick handfuls of leaves and outbursts of flowers.
For the first time in Nassau we felt like we had found someplace
we recognized. The day was steadily getting hotter, the sun
pale with its own iridescence, but a short way down the hill
we found a white stucco building, the entrance closed with an
old wooden gate, and a sign reading 'guest house'.

We were certainly as much out of place when we knocked
at the gate as we had been at the formal dinner on the ship the
night before, but we were as certain that we would be more
comfortable here. There was a small bar inside the gate, pale
in muted shadows and deep in stillness. Two men were talking with the midday's desultory ease. There was no hurry for
them to finish their conversation, since doing anything else

besides sitting and talking would mean going outside into the sun. One of them was tall, his face a weathered shade of brown. The shorter man was darker-skinned, wearing a white shirt that gave his skin a black sheen. His face had been sculptured and smoothed by the wind, and his eyes were wrinkled from years of sunlight. The tall man was wearing a hat, which meant he'd come in from the street, and it must be the shorter man who ran the guest house.

'Yes,' he stood up slowly. 'Yes, there is a room.'

When he came a few steps toward us he looked at us a little more closely, as if he were unsure what we wanted the room for. I could see him looking at our poor clothes, at the worn bags and the suitcase, the clumsy tape recorder. We were too obviously shabby to be doing anything dishonest, since even the most inept kind of dishonesty would have to pay better than whatever it was we were doing. He shrugged and pointed to a staircase at the front of the bar.

'If the room pleases you, you can stay.'

With a careful discretion he never asked us where we had come from or what we were doing, even months later when we came back into his shadowy bar with our skin brown from the sun and our hair bleached from the sea and our clothes and bags looking even shabbier.

The door to the room up the rickety staircase was as darkly shadowed as the bar downstairs, but there was a lacing of wooden slats over the windows, and the white glare of the sun threw sharp contrasts across the worn floorboards. The room was a pattern of vivid lights and shadows cast across the room and the floor in a complicated abstract design. The shapes had made their own unconscious patterns. It was a room that didn't seem to need people in it, but when we piled our things up against the battered dresser and lay down on the narrow beds to let the heat drain out of us, the stripes of light slowly climbed up from the floor and inched their way across the sheets toward us, as if they were

curious to see what it was that had interrupted the stillness of the day.

We had no idea how we would get to Andros, but for the rest of the day it didn't matter. We'd come closer. We could sense that in the smells and the sounds of the streets around us. We went downstairs an hour later, and found the owner of the guest house and his friend still sitting in the bar. We ate a sandwich, nodded in agreement when they said it was too hot to go outside, but after a moment we looked at each other and grinned wildly and decided we had to go out anyway. We were too excited to be in Nassau to stay inside. Ann climbed the narrow stairs again and came back down with our bathing suits and towels. She asked where we should go to swim, and the men laughed softly and suggested that she go and look for the water.

Even in the heat the crowds of tourists had grown along Bay Street and there was a crush of traffic, a smell of exhaust fumes, and a noisy din of voices from the cruise ships. For us, though, none of this made the sun less golden or the sky a murkier blue, and through the crowd of boats we could see that the water still shone blue-green in the channel beyond the beaches.

The beaches, the shining white beaches, we soon learned were owned by the hotels, and it wasn't possible to use them unless you were a guest. That was why the men in the guest house had been evasive when they answered Ann's question. When we asked the people who were selling the tourists hats and wood carvings and printed shirts where people like us could swim they pointed further down the street. There was a beach there and anybody could go in the water. It was a walk of nearly a mile in the sun, but at the end of the walk there was a beach that was open to the people of Nassau. We took off our shoes and walked gingerly onto the stinging sand. In the glaring sun there was an intermittent, swaying movement to the waves and a sheen of heat to the water that bound it in a close relationship to the sun, just as the night before on the ship the water had been bound in an embrace with the moon. But it wasn't a time to swim. It was too hot. There were only a handful of people on the beach. Speedboats churned up the sea close to the beach, and beyond them was a commotion of cruise ships. We could come back when it was quiet. The hotel beaches, stretching away beside us, marked off with their gleaming jetties and hemmed in with their shark nets, looked like a line of pools in a fish hatchery. Despite the din the beach where we were standing at least was open to us. The other beaches were closed, not only to us, but to the life of the town around them.

After sunset, when the sounds died away and the crowds thinned out along the streets the presence of the sea drifted in over the city. Its pungent smell hung even heavier over the dirt streets outside our small guest house. As it grew darker and darker we felt the water drawing us. Now Ann wanted to swim. We took our suits and went alone through the stirring shadows back to the beach where we'd stood in the afternoon. The trampled sand seemed to be empty, but clouds had drifted over the moon, and it was too dark to see more than a few feet. I wanted to feel the warmth of the sand so I sat down and let Ann go in the water without me. I stayed back against the line of trees at the edge of the beach, where the hanging vegetation cast everything into even murkier shadows.

As I was straining to see where Ann had gone into the water I was suddenly conscious of soft footsteps coming up behind me on the narrow patch of gravel that led from the road to the beach. It was so dark I could have been holding my hands over my eyes. I could hear the footsteps coming closer, but when I turned I couldn't see anything.

Could the other person see me, did they know we were there? I felt foolish and I was also afraid. I was sitting on an empty beach in the darkness, waiting for a girl to finish a lonely swim in the warm surf that lay in even deeper darkness just beyond me. She had called out to me a moment before I heard the footsteps. I couldn't leave her, even if I could find my way back into the shelter of the bushes. The sound of the footsteps stopped, and I could sense a figure standing a few feet from me. I started to get to my feet.

'Sir,' a voice said in a muted tone, 'Sir, is that someone you know swimming in the ocean?' The voice had a musical Bahamian accent.

'Yes,' I answered slowly. 'I know her.'

'Then you could tell her it not be safe to swim in the channel. When the noise from the boats go away at night then the sharks come.'

I straightened up, relieved that the voice was friendly, but even more frightened that Ann was swimming there in the water.

I managed to say some kind of thanks. I was looking through the darkness toward the place where she'd left her clothes.

'Tell her don't swim back too fast. The shark he listen for splashing.'

I began to hurry across the trampled sand. 'I'll tell her. Yes, I'll tell her.' I was whispering as if the sharks could hear me from the beach. The footsteps were already moving away across the gravel as I came to the edge of the water and waded into the swell with my shoes still on.

'Hey,' I began calling in a low voice, 'Hey.'

I was trying to keep my voice steady. It was impossible to believe that anything could happen to her. Not on such a warm, languorous night, just when we had come to the island. Her voice came back slowly across the muffled chop of the low waves.

'It's so beautiful. I can see the phosphorus. You come in too.'

'You should come in now.' I could hear that my voice was stiff, but I couldn't make my throat work.

'The water's perfect.' I could hear the faint sound of her arms moving in the water as she protested.

'But you should come in.' I added 'Please,' without thinking.

It was the 'Please' that made the difference. I didn't dare say anything else, since a frightened splashing would have been felt through the water by anything swimming close to her. She turned back toward the beach, swimming with her smooth, almost silent strokes, and it wasn't until she stood up and let the water drain off her that I heard a splash. She came toward me, rubbing the salt water out of her eyes.

'What is it?'

I began laughing, and for a moment I couldn't do anything else but laugh. I put my arms around her, not caring if my shirt got as wet as she was.

'A man just came and told me that at night the sharks come into the channel.'

She stopped, her feet suddenly dragging in the sand.

'You didn't tell me when I was in the water.'

'He said you shouldn't splash. You should swim in slowly.'

'Oh,' she said, 'Oh.' Her voice went up and even in the darkness I could see her eyes opening wide as she turned to look behind her at the sweep of foam at the water's edge. Then, arms around each other, we walked slowly back through the warm sand to the pile of clothes and the darker shadows of the road that led back to Nassau. Our summer had begun.

3

The Problem with Fishing Boats

The next morning, when we went to the small shipping offices and ticket agents along the waterfront, we found we still had a problem getting to Andros. There was a mail boat, a rusted, slow steamer, but it only made the trip once a week and it had left the morning we arrived. We could stay at our run-down guest house until the ship was ready to leave again, but that would take as much of our money as getting there any other way, and we were becoming impatient to finally get to the island and find some trace of the song that continued to haunt me. The travel agents we turned to weren't much more helpful than the ones we had talked to in Miami.

'Since you missed the mail boat it's going to be a week until it leaves again. I don't know what you'll do anyway when you get there. It's a empty place. At least that's what people say.'

Usually they ended their half-hearted suggestions for ways to get to Andros by trying to interest us in the tourist sites around Nassau.

'I know you'll find so much more to do here. If you take a sightseeing boat over to Paradise Island there are all the hotels and their beaches . . .' But when they saw the expressions on our faces they stopped talking.

The owner of the guest house had a few more customers after dinner, and an old man sitting alone at the bar overheard us talking about our problem. He made his way to the table and sat down stiffly in an empty chair beside us. The room was so poorly lit that we could only see the stripes of his shirt and his shining eyes.

'A fishing boat.' His voice, rough and unsteady, was insistent. We could always find a fishing boat to take us to Andros. 'You talk to the captain. He take you with them.'

The next morning we hurried out on the streets before the sun began to press its dead weight down on the day. We found the native fishing sloops tied up in an uneven line at a weathered pier further along the waterfront, beyond the area where the cruise ships anchored. The sloops were such a raffish sight that most of the tour guides led their customers there as well, and there were dozens of people from the cruise ships in their Bermuda shorts and freshly ironed golf shirts staring at the unkempt, muscular men of the fishing boats, who tried to pay no attention to the lenses of the cameras turned toward them.

It was our first close glimpse of the sloops, the boats that were to be part of our lives for the rest of the summer. They were crude and picturesque, like some kind of rough ship model that had been made to go inside a bottle, but then left outside to grow. They had been built by the fishermen themselves, working with hand tools on the beaches of two or three of the Out islands. They were constructed out of rough, unpainted planks; short, stubby hulled boats with a rounded, bottom heavy shape and shallow, broad sails that were in as torn and ragged condition as the fishermen's torn shorts and dirt blackened pants. The deck timbers of the boats had bleached a dirty gray with the unending sun, but usually the names were painted on the stern, and the painted names were fresher.

The small boats — they were about thirty feet long — rose and fell sluggishly in the water. They sat so low in the water because a compartment in the center of each boat — almost a third of the hull area — had been sealed off from the rest of

the hull and then holes had been drilled in the bottom so the sea water could flow through the compartment. It was a living well for their catch of fish. Anything the crew caught was dumped in the well through a hatchway on the deck and the fish would stay alive there until the boat came into harbor. Since the boats had no facilities for refrigeration, or even for drying fish, this was the only way they could deliver their catches.

The weight of the water pouring in and out through the hole in the bottom gave the ships a stolid gait in the wind, and they rested on the agitated swells of the harbor with the same heavy resignation. If they had to move they did it unwillingly. Tied to each other and to the long pier they looked as though they had settled there for good in a welter of frayed ropes, masts, slumped sails, and smells. The heaviest of the smells hanging over the line of boats was fish, but there was almost as strong a mingling of oil and exhaust from the small auxiliary motors mounted on the newer of the boats. There were also the smells of pigs and crates of chickens lashed to the decks of the sloops hoping to get out on the next tide. Hanging over everything was the smell of the sea. As we walked along the littered pier from boat to boat it seemed entirely natural that the sun should be streaming down so unmercifully, that the voices should be loud with annoyance and heavy laughter, and that everything should smell.

One of the boats, tied up half way down the line, was going to Andros. The captain nodded when we came up to him and asked if he was from the island. The term 'captain' simply meant that he was the owner of the boat and he hired the two or three men who worked the boat with him. He was a tall, black-skinned man with red-rimmed eyes and unsteady hands. His face was narrow and lined, and a vein pulsed at his temple. He was wearing a wrinkled white shirt and dark trousers. His feet were bare. He pushed one hand into the waist band of his trousers, staring past us at the harbor as he

talked, as if it made him uncomfortable to look at our faces.
Yes, he was sailing in the middle of the night.

'When the tide, you know, he be right.'

It wasn't going to be tonight. He still had to pick up things
to take back with him. Tomorrow night. How long would it
take to get across? He thought about it, stared across the
water again and he shrugged.

'Sometime we come there fast. Sometime it take longer.'

We agreed on a price — very low — and the three men of
the crew who would be sailing with us looked up at us
curiously from the deck of the boat. They were in the same
tattered clothes as the rest of the crews along the pier, with
the same scarred hands and the same lines creased into their
faces from the sun. They slept out on the deck — we would
sleep on the deck with them. The boat didn't have a toilet.
There was a small wooden frame filled with dirt in the middle
of the deck for the cooking fire. But if the captain was right
the boat 'could be there fast.' If the winds were right it
wouldn't be a long sail. It wouldn't be too hard for us on the
boat. The captain and I shook hands and we agreed again that
we would meet the next night. The tide would be going out
sometime close to midnight. We would bring everything to
the boat and we would see him then. The crew stared at us
steadily, one of them waved, and we went back along the pier
to get out of the sun's swelling glare.

Captain Kelly. I can still remember his name after so many
years when I've forgotten so many things that are much more
important, and his nervous, bloodshot eyes and his shaky
hands are still there in my memory. . . .

The next night, as we picked our way slowly back to his
boat, weighed down with our bags and suitcases and the tape
recorder, nothing along the pier was teeming. A few sleeping
dark figures lay there or on the boat decks wrapped in light

blankets. There was no sound of a voice and the night wind had driven off some of the smells. It was almost lifeless. There was a scurrying in the shadows, but it wasn't the kind of movement we had seen in the sunlight. Everywhere along the pier there was the scurrying, scratching sound of harbor rats as they ran on and off the decks and ducked under the hatches of the shadowy boats. In the daylight the cargoes and the patched boats and their crewman had seemed so poor that it was almost inconceivable that there could be anything left over for any other kind of creature, but to the rats these weathered boats and their ragged crews were an inexhaustible store of food and shelter and we could make out their dark, large shapes as they crept around us.

Captain Kelly, on the other hand, didn't seem to be there. His boat was tied where he'd left it, sliding up and down against the pier with a yawning, groaning sound as the damp boards rubbed against the peeling cement, but there was no sign of life around it. We put down the bags and suitcases and bundles we'd been struggling with, now with the added weight of a bag of food we'd bought to take on the boat with us, and I stumbled along the pier, looking for a way to clmb down onto the shrouded deck. A figure in a pale blanket stirred against the hatchway. It was one of the boat's crew.

'He not come now. He be in town. He drunk.'

'When will he sail?'

The crewman made a motion inside the wrapping of his blanket. He had probably shrugged, but it was difficult to see much more than the outline of the blanket and his dirty canvas shoes. If the whole scene hadn't been so dream-like we would have been frightened, alone on a rat-ridden pier in the middle of the night. Our innocence again had left us stranded. But the crewman only seemed sleepy.

'I think the tide, he be right tomorrow night. Maybe some night after that.'

He pulled the blanket up around his shoulder again and curled up against the hatchway.

In the vague darkness the worn planks of the boat's deck looked a little like the rounded back of a fish, the mast with its sagging sail like a large fin. The shadowy line of boats was like a school of swollen dolphin nudging against the pier, and we could hear the monotonous splash of water against their sides. We picked up our bundles and suitcases and started back toward the distant gleam of the first street lamp at the end of the pier, feeling as though we were swimming ourselves, but swimming through a current of shadows instead of the swell of the current below the boards of the pier. Around us we could hear the sound of the rats again, their feet whispering as they wavered on the swaying lines that held the dim, humped forms of the boats nosed in against the pier.

When we'd gotten half way to the light we heard uneven footsteps and with some of the nervousness of the rats we drew back against some stacked boxes. In the faint stream of light coming from the street lamp I could see that it was Captain Kelly. I took a step out of the shadows to say something to him, but I could see that he was as drunk as his crewman had said he would be. He wasn't going to be sailing anywhere for the next few days. We picked up our luggage again and struggled toward the street lamp.

Our arms were aching and we were streaked with perspiration when we came back down the darkened street that led toward the closed gate of our guest house. We didn't know if anyone would let us in, or if we even still had a room, but there was a light on in a side room downstairs. After a few minutes of knocking the gate was slowly pulled open enough for the owner to look out. He had done his best to discourage us when we had told him we were going to sail on a sloop to Andros. He didn't seem at all surprised to see us standing tired and dirty again on his doorstep.

*

When we finally woke up the next morning we shook off our stiffness and our discouragement and went to the beach to lie in the sun and try to decide what to do. After our first days of asking at shipping offices and travel agents along Bay Street we knew almost everything there was to know about crossing the sixty miles of ocean that lay between us and Andros, but our knowledge didn't add up to much. There was the mail boat, and it still wouldn't be back for a few days, and there were the fishing boats. We could go back to the pier and try another captain. Ann had already been swimming, and she was lying on a towel drying off. She stretched her arms and looked at her hands.

'The boats looked so small when we got there last night.'

We thought about it. The boats had looked very small when we stood there in the shadows beside them. How long would we have to spend on one of the sloops, if we could find one that would sail to Andros? What did the men in his ragged crew mean when they said the winds had to be right?

We sat up on the towels we'd spread on the sand, talking so steadily we didn't notice the beach slowly filling up around us. We had to do something before we spent all our money in Nassau. We were caught in the same dilemma that had faced us in Miami.

We had also been told that if we had the money for the tickets there was a plane. Around the islands there always seemed to be small planes that made short trips. The plane flew to a settlement on Andros called Fresh Creek, on the northern half of the island. We spent an age adding up our money and trying to decide if we could take the plane and still have enough left to live when we got to Andros. The sun faded away and layers of clouds pushed into a darkening heap over our heads as we talked and talked, trying to decide what to do. Children rushed up to stare at our strange faces, at our

hair and pale skin, then backed shyly away. Still talking we
waded into the water, putting the problem out of our minds
as we dove under the eddying green surface, and it was only
when we came up for air and shook our faces free of the taste
of salt that we felt the first tentative drops of rain.

At first we kept on swimming, then a distant suggestion of
thunder drove us back to the beach. As we stood back at the
edge of the sand under a tree we were joined by people in
various stages of dress and undress who hurried to take shelter
with us, all of them Bahamians who stood self-consciously a
few feet away from us despite the crowding to get some
shelter from the abrupt rain. Soon after we'd reached the trees
there was a deafening crash of lightning against the water,
and we all pressed together under the scant protection, staring at the spot where we'd been swimming a few minutes
earlier. Through the gray cascades of rain we could see one of
the native sloops, like the one we had tried to take to Andros,
two hundred yards away from us in the middle of the channel.
The sails hung as slack as a wish no one expects to be fulfilled,
the men on deck huddled close to the hatchway with sodden
pieces of canvas held over their heads. Without a direction to
the wind the boat drifted slowly with the current. It had no
motor, and it was unable to sail out of the harbor. We looked
at each other wide-eyed and despairing. The question of how
to get to Andros had been decided for us.

The next day was clear and hot again. The few clouds were
distant piled puffs of white. If we hoped to leave Nassau in
the next few days the plane was the only alternative. It was
time to get to Andros and begin working. Downstairs the
owner of the guest house had moved the tables back against
the wall and he was sweeping the room. He only nodded
when we came down the narrow stairs again with our bags
and suitcases. We were so obviously young and inexperi-
enced, and since we were staying at his guest house we were
certainly poor, so he no longer seemed perturbed by anything

we did. He was wearing one of his white shirts again, the sleeves rolled up, and he stopped with his broom to watch us as we said a self-conscious goodbye and went out into the sunlight.

The plane was very small, and it felt as unsteady as the deck of Captain Kelly's sloop. The plane swayed down the runway, then became airborne with an abrupt lurch, as if someone had finally picked it up and given it a push. We were strapped into the two passenger seats on either side of a narrow aisle, but we could see out through the small windows of the cabin, and whatever hesitations we had about the plane, the scene below us was worth whatever we would have to pay for it.

The plane arched up over the uneven edge of the beach and out over the deepening, shining blue of the water. The water was so clear it was as though we could see completely through it, but the color itself had its own substance. It was so blue that it seemed it might be possible to dip your hands in it and watch them turn the same blue tone. First we lifted above the light blue of the shallow water, where the sand underneath it gave it a translucent gleam, a kind of pearly luminosity from within. Then the pale blue darkened to a blue-green, as if there were a growth of sea plants on a sliding shelf of land reflecting its presence up to the surface. Beyond that was the rich, dark blue of the channel that swept between the islands. It was a blue that had the depth of rubbed stone, and the iridescence of its surface was set off in a quavering relief by the white crowns of the running swell of waves that pushed across the surface of the water in glistening lines.

In the channel we could also see small fishing boats trying to make their way to Andros. Their sails hung with a dispirited, flapping lifelessness. We looked at each other across the plane's narrow aisle. If Captain Kelly had sobered up enough in time to take us on his boat we would be there on one of those sun-flooded decks, becalmed in the stifling heat. We sat back in the cramped seats, letting the plane take us where it wanted.

We still knew so little about Andros that we didn't have any expectations of what it would look like. From the air the sea reversed its arrangement of hues, its blue tone becoming lighter and lighter until the whiteness of the long curve of beach finally lifted out from it. The land behind the beach was mostly flat and featureless; a rough surface of dun-colored earth covered with an uneven texture of small plants. There were only a few scattered large palms. The growth was short and stubbly and as the plane settled down onto the short runway constructed out of a thin covering of crushed sea shells we could see that most of the vegetation was a scrim of low, spiny bushes.

I'm certain that Andros has changed since we landed on the narrow dirt runway so many years ago. Almost every place else on the Earth has changed since then. There are so many more of us than there were then, and we need so much more of the Earth now. But that afternoon on the island we found only the beginnings of the first thin veneer of the tourism that had turned Nassau into a noisy, crowded caricature of itself. The veneer consisted of a thin, nervous white man in carefully ironed slacks and a dress shirt who wasn't any older than we were, standing on the gritty dirt with two black workers beside a dusty car waiting for us. No one at any of the travel bureaus had thought to tell us that there was a hotel at Fresh Creek, the first one on Andros. It had been open a little more than a year, but summer isn't the season for tourists on most of the islands. The man worked at the hotel and he'd gotten a radio message from the pilot of our plane that two passengers were on the way over. He was expecting us to stay at the hotel and he motioned for the workers to pick up our luggage. I said no, we knew from the map we had with us that there was a native settlement on the other side of Fresh Creek and we just wanted to get to the settlement.

The man looked confused. He ran his fingers through his hair. The workers with him paid no attention to either of us. 'You have some place to stay there? You know anybody there?'

'No.' I was holding on to the tape recorder with both hands. I hadn't let the two men touch it.

'You mean you don't want a room at the hotel?'

'No.' To keep the afternoon pleasant we were both smiling.

'Do you know what's over there in the settlement?'

'No,' I admitted.

'There isn't anything over there. It's just where the natives live. You won't find anything over there, and even if you do find anything you won't like it very much.'

He was uncomfortably anxious to get us to his hotel, but at the same time he was trying not to say something that would offend his two workers, who had finally begun to watch the exchange with amused expressions.

'The hotel has some rooms,' he added. It was obvious that the hotel had many rooms and all of them were empty. Ann and I shook our heads, standing where we had stopped at the edge of the airstrip, our things heaped around us. It seemed even hotter than in Nassau. We were perspiring, but the stirring air dried our skin almost immediately.

'How far is it to the settlement?' I asked after an uncomfortable silence.

He looked away with an annoyed expression, then he gestured toward the car. 'I've got to go back anyway. You ride in with me, and the settlement's just across the creek. But . . . if you'd like to look at a room I can show you something.' It was obvious he still felt there was some hope for us.

'We've never been in a settlement,' Ann tried to explain.

He shrugged, the two workers lifted our things into the car's trunk, and we started off. The bumpy stretch of road that wrenched its way through the brush had been built only a short time before and it still had a temporary feeling to it, as if the brush were going to reclaim it. The sand was sifting back into the ruts and the tendrils of plants were creeping back across the cleared earth, despite the intrusion of the occasional car that ran over them on the way to the landing strip. As it turned out this was the only road we saw on Andros, and this rattling car was the only vehicle.

The new buildings that had been constructed along the south bank of Fresh Creek were still so inconsequential that we could take everything in at a single glance. There was the cluster of the hotel outbuildings, small stucco structures for tools and storage, and the low, blocky shape of the two-story hotel itself. A half-hearted stretch of garden set it off from the indifferent tangle of the brush we had just driven through. Beyond the hotel was the gleaming surface of Fresh Creek and across the creek — which was about fifty yards wide — were the scattered small houses of the settlement. We could see a few newer houses close to the edge of the ocean at the mouth of the creek across from us, but they were the only intrusion. The one-story, wooden frame houses of the settlement, what we could see of them through the fringe of trees and brush, and the weathered stucco church at the water's edge looked like they had been there for many years. When we told the man from the hotel again that we didn't want to look at a room he pointed toward the bank of the creek. Built out into the water was a small wooden dock that functioned as a boat landing.

'That's how you get across.'

He looked at us again, then he lifted his shoulders in resignation.

'Should be a boat there — it'll take you over. Then the man can bring you back here after you've had a look around at what the places are like to stay over there.'

We thanked him, picked up our things, and walked slowly toward the landing, passing an open-fronted shed that had a scarred counter and shelves of what looked in the dimness to be canned goods for sale. A weathered open row boat was tied to the landing, with a single long sculling oar protruding over the stern. A man who looked about twenty years old, with shining black skin and arms that bulged below a shirt with sleeves torn away, stood up from the place against a shed where he'd been resting in the shade and climbed into the boat to wait for us. He had a large, broad face with a thick jaw, and he had let his matted hair grow long. When we pointed to the landing on the other side of the creek he nodded and grinned and picked up the long oar.

We were to make so many more trips back and forth across Fresh Creek in the small boat, but on this first trip what surprised us was the strength of the current flowing out toward the ocean only a few hundred yards from us. We got used to the current, but we never could get used to the experience of seeing the shine of the sun on the water and hearing the glistening splash of the sculling behind us. Looking over our heads the man stood behind us in the boat, sculling away from the little dock with a rocking, twisting motion that slowly propelled the boat forward. The current was carrying us toward the mouth of the creek, but with what was clearly long practice he'd pointed the boat upstream when he'd sculled away from the dock and as he pulled the oar back and forth the prow of the boat stayed pointed toward the trampled mud of the bank where he was to pull up on the opposite shore.

When we carried our suitcases and bags and the tape recorder up the low mud bank and stood looking around us at the worn little wood frame buildings and the rough hand-tilled gardens we felt that we finally had gotten through the last shreds of the encroaching veneer of Nassau and Miami. We had at last come to a place that was different — different because in most of the ways that mattered it was only itself.

4

An Island House

There was so much that surprised us about that summer —
so many things happened that we didn't expect. But for the
first few days I think we were as much of a surprise to the
people of Fresh Creek as they were to us. As we climbed up
the creek bank we could see a group of men in striped shirts
and work pants sitting in the shade of a primitive bar at the
edge of a clearing under some palm trees. They were playing a
noisy game of checkers that involved slamming the pieces
down on the board as hard as they could and jeering loudly at
each other when they made a move. As we came toward them
there was an abrupt silence. The man who was about to slam
his checker on the frayed board stopped with his arm raised,
staring at us. Trying not to appear too uncomfortable I hurriedly asked if Fresh Creek had a District Commissioner, and
where could we find him. The shipping offices in Nassau had
told us that the settlements on Andros were under the super-
vision of a District Commissioner, and the Commissioners
could answer any of our questions.

One of the men stood up from the game, put on a stained
straw hat to keep off the sun, and began to walk away,
stopping when he'd gone a few feet to make it clear that he
was waiting for us to follow him. Heaving our things up off
the dusty earth of the clearing we followed him along a
meandering path that led through the brush close to the
creek, taking us back toward the ocean.

The District Commissioner had been given a large stucco house on the headlands that hung above the water. We trailed behind the man who was leading, and he stopped on the path so we could go ahead without him. The District Commissioner was just as surprised to see us on his doorstep, but since he realized he was expected to meet the occasional strays who might drift through Fresh Creek he smiled nervously and asked us what we wanted. He was from Nassau, in his early twenties, and it was soon obvious that Fresh Creek was his first job. We also soon learned that he had just come back from Nassau on a motor boat and his wife had become hopelessly seasick and she was lying in the next room while we talked. He was thin and light-skinned, with short, tightly curled hair. His face was as thin as the rest of him, and he watched us uncomfortably from the other side of the bare room. We were becoming conscious of the gradations of skin color around us, since everyone we talked to identified everyone else by the color of their skin. We usually forgot that we were the palest of all the people on the island, and we would become conscious of it again only when someone looked surprised to see us.

The Commissioner was as surprised as the man from the hotel that we didn't want to stay across the creek in one of their empty rooms. We explained that we wanted to be on this side of the creek, with the people of the settlement. I lifted the tape recorder and talked about the song I had heard from Andros and he looked a little less uncertain, but he was from Nassau, and he'd never heard anything like what I was describing. We didn't say that we couldn't have stayed across the creek even if we'd wanted to. We didn't have enough money. If we had told him how little money we had he wouldn't have believed us. Our clothes looked too new — even if they were wrinkled and sweaty in the heat — and if we had really been poor we would have been much more worried about what would happen to us.

Was there any place to stay in the settlement? His face was stiff and expressionless while he thought about it. He clearly didn't know what he was supposed to do with us, and we didn't know how much he could do. There were probably less than a hundred people in Fresh Creek, and it wasn't as easy to find someplace to stay as we'd expected. In small villages like this there isn't much space left empty, since there's no reason to build something that isn't going to be used. But workers had been brought in from other settlements along the coast and from Nassau to build the hotel, and some of the villagers had built small houses to rent out to them. Now that the job was done the workers had left. The Commissioner thought there was an empty house close to the water, not far from the boat landing we had just left. An old woman in the village owned it. If we could find her we could ask her what she wanted for renting it.

As we went back down the path the Commissioner and the man who had led us to his house both came with us. It was still early afternoon, and it was blindingly hot in the sun, but so little happened in the village that we had become the day's diversion. As we passed the store beside the clearing the other checker-players pushed the checkers into a heap on the board and got up to straggle along after us.

The group of us came to a stop at the old woman's house, a yellow-painted board house back in the shadows under a clump of palms. She was very dark skinned, in a well washed, severely plain cotton dress; a thin, wiry woman with sharp eyes, her hair hidden by a faded bandana, a battered pipe between her lips. Unlike the others she seemed to sense that we didn't have any money. She studied us carefully, taking a step back and sucking at her pipe as she made a quick judgement of our clothes and our luggage. Finally she coughed and looked away, one corner of her pursed mouth turning up in what I was sure was amusement.

As we stood there in the dusty shadows under her palm

trees waiting for her to make up her mind I wondered what she thought of us. I suspected that for her it was less complicated than it was for the others in the village to decide what we were doing there. To the old woman it seemed obvious that since we were young, we were obviously in love, and if we wanted to live in a poor shack in a straggly village where the wind blew in the wrong direction we must be hiding from someone. Finally I think the entire village decided she was right. Who it was we were hiding from, I don't think they ever decided, but the women often seemed to be trying to help Ann, as if they wanted to let her know that they understood her situation and she had their sympathies. The old woman stared over the heads of the crowd that had gathered behind us, took her pipe out of her mouth, and told us that if we wanted we could move into the house she had by the creek. $14 a week. It was more than we had hoped we would have to pay. I hung back, hesitating. She shrugged, put the pipe back in her mouth and waited silently. I couldn't think of any other choice so I asked her if we could look at it and she turned silently, letting us follow her as best we could along the dry dirt path that led to the shack.

Native buildings throughout the world have a wonderful variety. They have a shape and texture that derive from the climate and the surroundings. They look like the plants or the mud, the trunks or the vines or the stones that are there for people to build with, and the huts take their form from whatever tools the people have learned how to use. Wooden shacks — on the other hand — all look pretty much alike. Boards only seem to go together in certain predetermined angles, and to make the floor level you have to build from the ground up. Usually there's some variety in what goes on the roof, since this reflects the current level of prosperity in the area more than it does the local setting. Probably everywhere

in the world the most common roofs are made out of corrugated iron, since it's the easiest and nearly always the cheapest roofing material to build with.

The little house she led us to fitted the usual description — small and square-shaped, with an angled roof of corrugated iron. It was, however, more elaborate than the usual board shack. There were front steps and a small, pleasant porch with a railing, and inside were two rooms, one set up as a kitchen with an electric hotplate and a worn wooden table and chairs. The other room, opening off the kitchen, was larger and it contained two iron bed frames and sagging mattresses. The little house's amenities ended with the one bedroom. There was no running water, no sink of any kind, no toilet, no bathroom. There was a board outhouse with a sagging door set in a thicket of bushes and palm shoots behind the house. The house itself had been painted a soft yellow at one time, like other newer houses in the settlement, but the wind and the rain had picked away at the paint until there was only a faint shading of it left as a reminder.

It was obvious that the house had been lived in by workers during the hotel construction, but it was clean and in fair repair. There were dangling bulbs and a wall socket so I could plug in the recorder and we could work after dark. We had a porch to sit on in the hot nights. We looked around again at the bare rooms, at the thin wooden walls and the shutters that took the place of windows, and looked at each other with hopeful expressions, then went outside again. The woman was still staring across the creek, her pipe clenched in her mouth, making it clear that she didn't care what we thought of her little house, or if we wanted to live in it. It was just as clear from the expressions of the other people from the settlement standing silently behind her that they hoped we would. We nodded, she and the Commissioner talked in low voices, and she bent her head, holding up her pipe with one hand, acknowledging that the deal had been concluded.

There was a path along the edge of the creek, and the little house — perched up on its cement block legs to lift it above the stony ground — was close to the path, less than a hundred yards from the boat landing. There was a wall built of heaped porous island stone at the edge of our yard, separating us from the path. We had three or four palm trees in the yard, some sparse grass, and a pepper bush. It looked like there had once been a garden in front of the house, but it had slid back to an unkempt barrenness. On the other side of the path, just opposite the opening in the low wall, there was a stolidly practical cement pier that projected a few yards out into the creek. Standing at the edge of the pier we could see down into the earth-tinged current, streaming from the shallows in the center of the island, and we could see striations of darting, glittering fish. We looked down into the world just below the rippled surface of the water for a moment, then we hurried back across the yard to our porch, too excited with the realization that we finally had gotten to Andros and we had someplace to stay to do anything more than move our things into the little house.

With the shutters propped open to get as much air into the cramped rooms as possible we went through bags and hung up clothes and spread out the books and the notes we had brought in our luggage. The walls were still bare, and the house was as worn and weatherbeaten as it had been when we'd first seen it, but for now it was a place we could live in, and we realized, suddenly laughing at each other, that we didn't have any other place to live. Fresh Creek was the only home we had.

The Commissioner had looked around the kitchen space and offered to lend us some pans. We were to come to his house and get them when it got a little cooler. That was the time that most things happened that summer — when it got a little cooler. People would tell us when we should come to talk to them, or when we should go off with them to fish, or when we should be ready to follow them to a boat — and we could finish the sentence for them. We would do it all when it got a little cooler. Over the long weeks we came to know the sun as well as we knew anyone else on the island. It was always there waiting for us, just outside the door, as if it had something it wanted to tell us, and if we just stood outside in the glare long enough it would remember what it was.

The day finally did get a little cooler. About four o'clock we walked slowly through the settlement. We wanted to pick up the pans the Commissioner had offered, we had to buy some food, we wanted to see what kind of place we had come to. There wasn't a lot to Fresh Creek. Thirty — perhaps forty — small houses, most of them wooden frame buildings like the one we'd rented. They straggled along the four or five paths that had been laid out in rough rectangles running parallel to the creek. A few of the houses had been stuccoed, and further along the creek was the first house built for an American owner who was planning only to spend a few weeks of the winter there. Probably now there are more of these houses, and probably now the native houses of Fresh Creek have been rebuilt as something else. The new house, with its shuttered windows, looked out of place on its bare patch of land. The other houses stood in the middle of a loose clutter of tools and toys and pieces of firewood and coconut husks and fishing nets.

   On our first walk we saw only a handful of people. Nearly everyone was out working. The men were in their boats or across the creek at the hotel, while the women were on the beaches, looking for shells, or in their garden plots. At the edges of the settlement was the same scraggly growth that covered most of the island — spiny bushes with tiny, unappetizing leaves, scrub conifers, and taller pines that edged the uneven horizon. There was a scrim of palm trees. The goats that scrambled out of our way made up for the lack of people. The large goats were usually tied close to the houses, but the small goats were everywhere. They were stringy, agile animals the color of dirt that seemed to roam freely, although they were more or less watched by all of the people in the settlement and they each belonged to someone. Along with the goats the settlement was filled with dogs. Nearly every house had at least one dog fastened close to the door. They were large, dirty, bristling, scarred mongrels. We were told that they were never allowed to come into the house. They were tied outside the house for noise and for protection. They were expected to fight anything that wasn't welcome in the yard. The families that owned them took considerable pride over their dogs' fighting abilities, and we often heard disparaging remarks made about the Commissioner's dog, which was a Nassau house pet, and with considerable intelligence refused to get into a fight with any of the dogs in the settlement. Most of the women also had chickens in their yards, but they kept them enclosed in small, fenced-in runways, and we heard the hens clucking to each other more often than we saw the birds themselves.

Even though the island was obviously dry and the soil was meager there was still a luxuriant growth around each house. The women brought water from the creek to splash on their plants and flowers. Often there were flowers dangling from the roofs or propped unsteadily against the house walls. Sometimes, however, what we thought was a flower turned out to be a large butterfly that clung to the end of a wavering stem, its wings slowly measuring the faint rhythm of its own fluttering.

The settlement had none of the noises of Nassau. There were no cars, no electric fans, no air conditioners, no motors of any kind, and without their level of sibilance we could hear the delicate tapestry of sounds that filled the air around us — the sounds of the birds, the wind rattling the dry palm leaves, the dogs perfunctorily snarling at each other, and the goats skittering across the paths on slender, hurrying hooves. There was little grass, a film of dust. Most of the ground under our feet was as hard as stone. We came to a large stucco building close to the creek — it was an Anglican chapel, with a small yard walled-off around it and a pier out over the water. The weathered door was locked and the plain windows closed and the building seemed to be so soundly sleeping that it was difficult to imagine it ever waking.

The few women who were out working in their gardens stopped what they were doing as we passed. There were smiles and nods. We were looking for some place to buy food, but the only shop the women could point out to us on our side of the creek was a house dark with overhanging vines and bushes. A front room had been turned into a little store. A large, shy woman in a tight, lemon-colored blouse and a wrinkled dark skirt stood behind the scarred counter and offered us cigarettes, canned milk, bars of soap, kerosene, fish-hooks, needles, thread, and dusty cans of corned beef. She didn't have any other food. We shook our heads and went outside. We would have to go back across the creek to the shed beside the hotel. Our movements, the movements of the sky and the air around us had become slow and languid, as though it were a matter of complete indifference whether or not we would find someplace to buy food. It wasn't only the heat that was affecting us, it was the casual disarray of the scattered gardens and the faint stirring of the birds. The goats were the only thing that moved quickly, and they seemed to be part of a different moment in time as they clattered past us through the spiny brush.

5

Night Voices

We usually walked along the paths in the early evenings, when the day had finally cooled down enough. There were different sounds in the lingering twilight. We could hear the voices of the families sitting around the dinner table. The dogs were quiet and the goats had crawled into the brush to sleep. There was no electricity in most of the houses, only kerosene lanterns that shed their muted yellow light. A few families had radios, but after the harbor news — which was the daily reading of the tide tables and the expected weather for every harbor in the Bahamas — most of the radios were turned off and people went to bed.

We were still so new to the village that we hadn't begun going to different houses to ask about songs, but the second night, as we walked slowly in the darkness along one of the paths in the middle of the village, we heard a distant, unsettled sound of singing. Sometimes the voices were in harmony, other times they broke off into shouts and exhortations, then for moments the tones would be scattered by the night wind. The songs seemed to be hymns — what we could hear of them — so we went down the path that led to the chapel by the creek, but its windows were dark and the door closed. The singing had to be coming from somewhere else.

Moving slowly and cautiously, feeling our way along the paths through unfamiliar breaks in the bushes and the low trees, we tried to follow the sound of the voices. We could see

almost nothing in the dimness, only the occasional outline of
a window where the kerosene lamp was still burning in the
room behind it. We didn't see as many people outside on their
porches. Fewer faces turned to follow us from the deeper
shadows — the murmur of talk behind the doors had almost
stilled. As we moved more and more slowly we began to see
other figures also walking toward the sound of the singing.
Most of the settlement seemed to be gathering somewhere in
a thicket that had been left to straggle along the headlands
above the ocean.

When we finally reached the clearing where the voices were
coming from we could see that the men and women were
gathered around another of the weathered houses. We couldn't
see the outlines of the roof or the porch, but the kerosene
lamps set on tables inside the main room flooded the windows with their golden amber glow, an essence of amber so
intensely pure that the faces and the furniture we could see
through the windows and the door could have been preserved
in its gleaming depths. But what were the voices, and why
were they singing? We stumbled through the litter of the
yard, edging closer, but we still didn't know why people had
gathered. From the wooden steps up to the porch we could
hear that the voices inside had begun another hymn, but
there were sudden emotional outcries of prayer, shouts, and
admonitions.

What had sounded like a ragged choir as we came through
the bushes separated itself into disparate elements of tone
around us. The voices inside the room were mostly those of
women, and we could see them sitting in a rough circle of
chairs, faces glistening with perspiration and tears, hands
jerking with spasmodic gestures as they shook out the hand-
kerchiefs they were pressing to their eyes. The voices on the
porches were men's. We could smell the coarse reek of rum,
and we could see the glint of the bottle as the men passed it
from hand to hand, drinking as they sang.

'You go in,' one of the men said unsteadily, 'you go in they find someplace you can sit.'

'What is the singing for?' I asked in a whisper.

The man drank again and shrugged. When he turned to look at us I saw that his face also was shining. He was crying.

'The woman in the house, she sick. She goin' die soon.'

We could make out the words of the hymn. Around us there were sudden outbursts of emotion.

> I be home, I be home in Jesus' breast,
> There to let me, there to let me rest.
> Take me to the Heavenly host,
> Glory be my soul at last . . .

> To thy refuge, to thy refuge, now I cling,
> Oh my helpless, oh my helpless soul I bring . . .

Then voices would interrupt: 'Hear me Lord, I'm praying to you, Oh Lord. . .' 'Oh Lord Jesus, I come to you, I'm thinking of you Lord Jesus . . .'

'We havin' a wake for her,' the man beside me said unsteadily.

'Is she still alive?' I whispered again.

'She die tonight maybe. Maybe tomorrow.'

It was difficult to see the expressions on the dark faces in the shadows of the porch. We could only make out the vague shapes of wrinkled shirts and trousers. No one had bothered to change their clothes when they got back to the settlement. The women inside the room were in their sun-faded house dresses or cotton skirts and blouses. Their hair was braided and pushed up under their straw hats. One of the women was reading the words for the song from an old hymn book that she held near a kerosene lantern. There were two or three men sitting on chairs pushed close to the wall, other men were bunched in the room's corners. Another woman, her head covered with a knotted red bandana, had turned toward the men sitting behind her and she was begging one of them to sing.

'John Roberts,' her voice was thin and hard with her grief, 'you must sing. You know it be time for you to sing. John, she listenin' for you.'

The man she had turned to was sitting in a worn, straight-backed wooden chair, its hand-carved, black-painted wooden slats almost as high as his head. He was slight and dark-skinned, with a fringe of white hair. His face was square and weathered, and when he looked up uncomfortably his eyes had a worried expression. He was wearing a white shirt with the sleeves rolled up and dark trousers. His body looked wiry and muscular, but in the room's yellow dimness what was most obvious was his embarrassment at being singled out. After his uncomfortable glance he stared down again at the boards of the floor.

'We must hear a song from you,' the woman persisted. Her voice was ready to break. 'You know she listenin', just like she always do.'

There was a darkened door at the end of the room, and the women kept turning to look toward the room beyond it, though there was no light inside. We realized that the dying woman was lying inside in her bed, listening to the voices.

John Roberts, the man who was being asked to sing, was obviously one of the settlement's best singers, but he was uncomfortable at being the center of the women's concern. Finally he straightened in the chair, leaned forward a little, still too self-conscious to look up from the floor. He cupped a hand against his ear to hear the pitch of the notes he was singing, and he began a hymn melody in a slow, strong voice. When he'd sung half a verse a second man joined in, a younger man whose face was lost in the shadows of the corner. He was bulky and broad shouldered, and his deep voice added a bass harmony to the Roberts's hymn melody. After another line of the verse a third man, younger than the first two, slim and light-skinned, joined them humming a high treble part, one hand cupped on his ear like Roberts, his eyes squeezed shut.

I couldn't name the hymn, but the melody and the simple harmonies were familiar. Suddenly, after they had sung two or three verses to be certain of the harmonies, Roberts stretched up in his chair, lifted his head, his eyes tightly closed, and he began to sing more freely and emotionally, creating a spontaneous variation of the melody and improvising a text that was built on the original words of the hymn in a complex rhythmic counterpoint to the voices of the other two men.

This was the singing that the people in the settlement had been waiting to hear. Men crowded around us on the porch. The women inside the room leaned closer to the singers, pulling their chairs around to hear better. Breathless at what we were hearing, Ann and I pressed closer to the window. As Roberts went on with his improvised verses the other two singers began to improvise on their own melodies. The basic harmonies of the song held the voices together, but their improvisations around the melody began to wind and unwind around each other with an intensity that seemed to become almost visible inside the room, as if the voices had turned into strings of light that were playing an intricate game of cat's cradle in the golden shadows. After a few more verses there was a subtle change in the intensity of Roberts's singing, and without turning his head to motion to the other two singers, at the next verse he went back to the simple melody where he'd begun. But they had sensed the shift, and without hesitating they slipped back into the standard harmonic cadences. The three voices ended on a basic triad, as if they'd done nothing more than perform the song from the notes in the hymn book.

For a moment there was a silence. Ann and I began breathing again, then two or three of the women began to pray together in thin, uneven voices. Out on the porch there was the dull glint as the bottle of rum was passed around again.

'What was that song?' I whispered to the man closest to me at the window.

'Just ordinary, no special,' he answered thickly.

'But the way they sang it?'

'That be rhyming,' the man shrugged. 'John just rhymin' it up.'

John Roberts stayed inside the room for a few more minutes, wiping his face with a large handkerchief, then he slipped away into the darkness before we could say anything to him. We kept our place at the window, despite the mosquitoes that had found all of us, but there were only prayers now, and if someone began to sing a hymn they faltered after a few lines and began praying again. We whispered goodnight to the people around us, slowly found our way down the steps of the porch and picked our way back along the darkened path.

Twenty years later, when I was using a much newer tape recorder to record singers in West Africa, I finally understood what it was I had been hearing in African-American music in the United States; in the blues, in gospel song, in jazz and ragtime — and now in Bahamian rhyming. African music has no strong rhythmic stresses — it has a rhythmic flow, and voices become part of the textural weave. Vocal melodies are freely interspersed with comments and changes of emphasis. African melodies use five-note scales instead of the western eight-note scale, so there is no distinctive minor mode.

What we had heard in John Roberts's singing was a shadow of an African past superimposed on the simple melody of the Anglican hymn. His rhythmic shifts had altered the European metronomic pulse of the hymn and given its melody some of the unstressed freedom of an African chant. The rhyming had become a kind of chant in itself. As the three voices had improvised together they had extended the simple harmonies of the hymn into a richer tonal palette than would have been possible in the notes in the hymnal. They had subtly shifted the structure of the hymn into a more complex modal form that reflected the stubborn memory of the different African scales. Even in this small black settlement on the coast of an island isolated on the western edge of the Atlantic Ocean the people still reached back instinctively to an almost forgotten heritage that still shone through the complex imposition of everything else that had happened to them in the centuries since Africa had been their home.

Roberts, however, was only conscious that his rhyming was an old way of singing. We found him late the next afternoon at his house, a two-room wood frame building not far from ours, but closer to the mouth of the creek. He was as spare and diminutive as he had looked through the window the night before, but his arms were wiry and muscular and his body was as hard as a board. His face still had its worried expression, and he seemed just as serious as he had been at the wake. He stood on the porch of his little house looking down at us with guarded curiosity. He had just crossed the creek with the ferry man. He was one of the handful of men who still had jobs at the hotel. He worked in the garden. When we told him how excited we had been by his singing the night before he shifted uncomfortably.

'That woman, she still livin',' he said. 'But she can't last long. She be a friend to everybody.'

When I asked him if he would record for us he shook his head emphatically. He still didn't think of himself as a singer.

'No, it not be right for me to sing for you. Frederick McQueen, now, Frederick McQueen could do it for you. He be the one to sing for you.'

It was the first time we heard the name Frederick McQueen, but we were to hear it again and again. The summer finally became a search for Frederick McQueen, but when John first said his name it meant nothing to us. As much to keep John talking as anything else I asked him about McQueen. Frederick was his cousin — we had already learned that nearly everyone on Andros was somehow related to everyone else — and he was a great singer. He was the greatest they had on the island all the time that John knew about singing. But I was less interested in McQueen. I was interested in John himself. I told him again that what we had heard him sing the night before at the wake had sounded very exciting to us. Did he know any more songs? Not knowing how to reply he stared down at the boards of his porch, then he looked away across the clearing toward the creek, as if he still wasn't sure what we wanted.

'That just be rhymin', what you heard.'

We had come all the way to Andros to find someone who could sing 'Dig My Grave'. Was that one of his songs?

He looked surprised. 'I know it,' he conceded finally. Could he come and record it for us, I persisted. He looked even more uncomfortable.

'I must have some of the boys sing it with me,' he said finally. 'You see, the old songs, they take more than one man. You got to have help.'

What about the boys who had sung with him at the wake? He became even more ill at ease. I was now asking him to involve other people in the idea of recording for us. Would they think the whole idea was as incomprehensible as he did? What did we really want from them?

What I began to realize after we had talked with John for a few days was that we had come into the settlement at Fresh Creek at a time of deep changes and confusions. The building of the hotel had brought in people from outside, there was music streaming in over the radio, there were still two businesses in the settlement that had places for dancing and juke boxes. A struggle was being waged over the music of singers who were part of an older tradition, like John, and it was a struggle over more than music. It was about a culture, about a way to live. When people like Ann and like me came into a community and tried to tell people what we wanted from them, we became a confusing new weight thrown on the scales of the delicate cultural balance. It wasn't a role that we wanted, but it was thrust on us, whether we wanted it or not.

What I was asking John to do was step forward and present his music — a music that he was being pressed to forget by the younger musicians who drifted through the settlement. For someone like him there was no thought of a musical career. He never thought he was being 'discovered', since in the life he knew there were only poor people who didn't own their own boats, and rich people who did. What he would do for us wouldn't buy him a boat. Did he even want to present himself as a singer in the old way, singing the old songs? I could see all of this turmoil going on behind his dark, serious face as he stood talking with us on his porch. He was obviously considering whether or not his neighbors would think he was vain if he recorded for us, or if they would murmur disapprovingly that he must think his songs are better than the songs the other people in the settlement knew. Like all native musicians he had painfully mixed feelings of pride over his singing and its traditions, and embarrassment over what he knew was the judgement of his younger neighbors of his kind of music. Sometimes when I thought about all the confusions and hesitation that I presented to someone when I asked them to record for me I was surprised that they did it at all.

John went on talking, but I could see his thoughts were weighing all the possible interpretations he could put on our visit. I had offered him money to record, but the amount of money itself wasn't large enough for that to be a factor. I always paid everybody who recorded something, and left them with an agreement that there would be royalties if I was able to find someone who would release their music on record, but the payment itself was almost ceremonial. For John, however, it legitimized the whole situation. I was asking him to do a job for me, and I was offering to pay him something for doing it. We could all understand each other on those terms.

John still hesitated, however, even as he nodded his head at what I was saying.

'Those two boys, you know, they can sing a little. And for the old songs it can't be just one. You have to have the bass and the treble to make it right.'

John was still wary of us, but as he looked down at us from his porch we certainly didn't look dangerous in our faded T-shirts and shorts, our faces shining with our first sunburn.

'I could pay them something,' I offered.

John stood thinking, nodding his head. If all he was doing was offering the other two a job he wasn't asking them to decide what kind of music they wanted to make themselves, or what kind of a new society they wanted to see at Fresh Creek. He was only offering them a job. He nodded his head again, this time a little more decisively.

When we had asked women in the settlement how to find John's house they had told us that he was an old man, but as he talked I could see that despite his gray hair he was still a young man, filled with enthusiasm and pleasure. Over the weeks we knew him we learned that as a boy he'd worked on the sponge boats, then when the sponges had disappeared he'd become a fisherman. But it was hard to make a living fishing, since there were fish everywhere in the ocean around the islands. The sloops from Andros wallowed to Nassau with their catches of fish crammed into the wells built into the boats' hulls, but when the money from the catch was divided up and the debts were settled there wasn't enough money for anyone to make any kind of decent pay for their labor. John, like the other men in the settlement, had worked on the other Andros projects; the pineapple farm, then the lumber mill until it burned down, and now the hotel.

He was also uncomfortable about calling himself a singer, because Fresh Creek was like an isolated community in the back country of the United States a hundred years ago. People in the settlement still made their own music. Everyone he knew sang, but there was only one man he knew that he would call a singer, and that was McQueen.

As he continued talking, however, I could sense that he was becoming more comfortable with the idea of recording for us. He had come down the steps of his house and he was standing out on the bare ground of his little yard. The light was fading and it was the moment in the evening when the mosquitoes were most vicious and the three of us shifted from one foot to the other, waved our arms in the shadows, slapped at our necks and faces — and at the same time he wanted to continue what he was telling us.

'They be so many of the old songs.' I could even hear a little excitement crowding against the shyness in John's voice. 'I know many, many of the old ones — but the young boys here, they sing, but they don't know the old songs. Now if Frederick was here he could sing them all for you. Frederick, now, he know them all.'

The mosquitoes were relentlessly driving us across the clearing and along the path. Without thinking about it we were moving a step at a time, still occasionally waving our arms, still listening to John talk, but walking in the direction of our own house. He followed us a few steps behind. He was too self-conscious to talk much about himself, but telling us about McQueen meant that he could talk about the old songs. What he said about his cousin and his importance in their small society also applied to himself. For John, a little of Frederick's reflected glory was as bright a light as he could bring himself to enjoy.

He realized that we still didn't understand what the man I had spoken to at the wake had meant when he used the term 'rhyming' to describe the intricate three-part counterpoint the three singers had improvised, with John creating a new text as he sang. John carefully tried to explain.

'A rhymer, see, he rhyme it up, while he singing. Whatever the song is about the rhymer he use that to tell a story, and he rhyme up more about it all the time the singing goes on. That's what the young boys don't know how to do. They don't know how to rhyme. Now the rhymer, he can't do it all alone. He just singing the ground, and he have to have the afterbeat from the others that's singing.'

As John talked his low voice with its flowing Bahamian dialect was almost lost in the splashing current of the creek and the scrabbling of the animals and chickens in the houses we were passing in the deepening shadows. I could feel again, as I had felt at the wake, the depths of time that had molded this small community in its isolation. 'Ground' was a musical term from another century. It had been part of the musical vocabulary from an earlier period when one melody — often called the ground — was the base on which the other melodic voices developed in a multi-voiced — a polyphonic — texture. The term John used for his songs was also an older one, 'anthems', instead of hymns. When he spoke about the newer songs he called them 'spirituals', and he referred to the principal melody as the 'lead', as we would today. Many of the terms had obviously survived through the old Anglican hymnals, but like most artists in an aural tradition John had clear and definite ideas about the nuances of style in the music he sang.

'Now Frederick, he sings the spirituals and the anthems, but it's when Frederick is doing his rhymin' that he take all the prizes.'

We had come to our house, and now our positions were reversed. We were standing up on the porch and he was in the scrabbly yard. He didn't want to come in. He 'had to have his sleep', but he still wanted to talk. Our long talk had obviously opened some kind of door for him, and he was unwilling to see it close so soon. Most of the mosquitoes had drifted away into the shadows and the yellow squares of light from the lanterns were dimming in the houses we could see through the wiry brush.

It was important for him that we understood about his cousin, and he began to tell us about McQueen again. They had grown up together in another indentation on the Andros coastline, a settlement called Blanket Sound about twenty miles north of Fresh Creek. They had worked together on the sponge boats, then when the fungus had killed the sponges they'd worked on the pineapple farm, and that was the last time he'd seen him, in 1940, almost twenty years before.

'But I hear he's still living. Sometime in Nassau, you know, the boats get tied up together and people talk to each other. If something happen to him I'd know, since he's my cousin.'

John finally had talked enough and he was ready to leave. When I asked again if he would come to the house and sing for us he nodded again, this time I could see him nod more emphatically. But he was apologetic. The old style singing needed those two other boys, but they didn't know the songs so well and he'd have to practise with them. How long would it be before they were ready? He thought a week would be soon enough, maybe two weeks, perhaps on a Sunday, when they'd all be back from their work. One day was as good as any for us, even if I could feel the familiar tug of anxiety and impatience at the thought of waiting to use the recording machine. He called goodnight, waved self-consciously, and stepped into the heavier shadows of the path. In the stillness after the murmur of his voice we stood on the porch for a moment listening to the sounds of the night — the muted surge of the creek, the distant sweep of the sea, a few lingering voices, the clank of a land crab somewhere under the house, and the abrupt whine of a mosquito close to my ear. Finally we groped our way into the clammy darkness of the little house and turned on the light in our bare-walled kitchen to see what we could find for supper.

6

Opinions About Sharks

In the endless, hot days at Fresh Creek the hours drifted past as we waited for John Roberts to get his songs ready for us. Since most of the people of the settlement were away working in their gardens or out on the boats, we could do what we wanted while we waited for them to come back. If we did find someone outside who looked like they'd been in Fresh Creek for many years, I asked them about Frederick McQueen. Even the woman who had rented her house to us smiled when I said the name. She took her pipe from her mouth and stated in a tone that clearly wouldn't accept any argument,

'That man could *sing!*'

The round-faced, plump woman who owned the little provisions shop on the other side of the settlement clasped her hands together when I said the name.

'Frederick McQueen! He could sing so beautiful. So beautiful! There'd never be a wake or a wedding that the people wouldn't come and carry him there to sing.'

I had left Ann in the house and I'd come to buy a packet of fish-hooks from her little stock so I could fish for our food. As I was going out into the sunlight she called after me that I should talk to Captain Johnson.

'He know about Frederick.'

Captain Johnson did know about Frederick, though, like John Roberts, he hadn't seen him for many years. He was an old man named Ormond Johnson, but he was still called 'captain,' since he had had his own boat during the sponging days. He was sitting inside his small, crowded front room when I came to his open door. McQueen had sailed as one of his crew more than twenty years before. I found myself looking at Captain Johnson's hands as he talked. His fingers, like those of most of the men in the settlement were worn and scarred, the joints still twisted and the skin cruelly indented from his years of hauling on lines. As he talked he rubbed his hands softly together, as if he were soothing old sores.

'We pull up at night on the sponge beds, you know. If it be really calm we let the boats come together, tied up so a man could walk from one boat to the other. But we didn't walk over to visit so much. We just want to be close.'

His voice was thoughtful and far away. He was clearly remembering something that was very precious to him.

'We run no lights. Only the coals still glowing red in that fire box out there on the deck and we be in our blankets because it be chilly in the night. Then we'd be lyin' there, looking up to the stars, you know, and Frederick would sing. I never heard anything so beautiful.'

Captain Johnson was a tough, worn man, and his dark face was almost as scarred as his fingers. He didn't seem sentimental about many things, but when he began to talk about his young days on the sponge boats he slapped his hands on his thighs, put his head back and laughed. The work had been grueling, they had made very little money for their labor, the primitive Andros sloops had been crowded and dangerous, but he remembered the moments at night, the silence of the sea. He slapped his thighs and laughed again.

'When we out there like that you feel like all you want in the world is there right in your hand.' He held up one of his battered hands and clenched his fingers, looking at me to see if I understood him. 'Right there!'

Did he think Frederick was still alive? Like Roberts, when I asked him the same question, he nodded immediately.

'We know it if something happen to him. Frederick, he be somewhere.'

In our first days in the settlement we couldn't have gotten along without our neighbors. Most of them were shy with us in the beginning The women mostly looked down at the ground, wiping their hands on their skirts. They wore wrinkled skirts and blouses, the older women usually covering their heads with a handkerchief and smoking a well-fingered pipe. It was the women who were helpful when we came to them to ask about the crabs. Our house had been built too close to the ground and the domed shells of the land-crabs banged against the floor joists as the crabs crawled under us on their way to the creek.

Land-crabs were everywhere. There was even one large one living in the bottom of our privy, and we could hear it scuttling noisily when it heard anyone approaching. No matter how often we saw the crabs in the daylight they were still dismaying. Or 'dismaying' is too bland a word for our feelings. The crabs were frightening. If we came too close to them they stopped and tilted their helmet-like, brownish bodies up on bent shanks of legs, following our movements with glittering small specks of eyes. The woman living in a house nearby said we didn't have to be afraid of them.

'They run,' she shrugged. 'They run if they see you too close.'

But if we were helpless on the ground, or sleeping?

She pursed her lips. 'So long as you can move. But you don't be lyin' too still if it be night out there.'

Sometimes people ate them, though they weren't popular as food. The woman said she ate them sometimes.

'We take 'em, keep 'em in the yard. You know why we do that. You don't know what they been eatin'. So we keep 'em in a fence and we give 'em scraps to eat so we know what they

got inside 'em. After two weeks they be clean. But you don't
eat 'em before that.'

A little uncomfortable at what we had seen them eat we
assured the woman we'd leave them alone. We slowly got
used to them, but when we encountered one and it stopped
and lifted itself up on stilted joints to stare at us we still took
an involuntary step back. The crab, its dirty shell blocking
the path in front of us, after a moment's inspection always
sidled hurriedly away.

When the men talked with us they stood almost as if they
were at attention, shoulders drawn back and hands awk-
wardly at their sides. They answered our questions about how
to store food or find light-bulbs, and told us what to look for
if we walked along the beaches or back into the brushy areas
to look for the small gardens. They worked the land as best
they could, but it wasn't very good land. They could work
small garden plots, but anything larger presented serious
problems. A few months later, when I looked for something
in a New York library about Andros I found an early description of the soil of the island where Nassau had been built, and
the sentences could have just as well been written about the
rough land around us on Andros. The man was a traveler
named Johann Schopf, who visited the islands in 1784.

> At a first view of this soil, everywhere rocky and stony,
> or of the white and dazzling sand by the shore, all notion
> of planting would seem to find contradiction, and all
> hope of a harvest from any plant quite beyond the possi-
> ble . . . An acre or piece of arable ground here has
> indeed a fearful look, for there is to be seen hardly
> anything but rock, full of larger or smaller pits and
> holes, containing a pretty strongly reddish earth. Nei-
> ther trenching nor plowing is therefore to be thought of
> — such spots may only be broken with a sharp mattock.
> It is no exaggeration to say that perhaps not the sixth,

nor the eighth part of the surface of the island is covered with earth, the rest being naked rock. However, in the wild state every spot is overgrown; the tree and plant roots creep over the rocks and stones, forcing into every cleft and hollow to find a lodging place and nourishment. It is clear that the native shrubs find merely a basis on the rock, and must draw their support chiefly from the air. On the coast there are to be sure large tracts free of rock; but its place is taken by dry shell sand in which the heat permits nothing to grow.

It was that ragged wild growth clinging to the burning rocks that hemmed the settlement in against the headlands of the ocean and the banks of the creek. When we tried to follow paths into the brush they soon petered out, leaving us in a maze of nearly impenetrable brambles, with small lizards peering up at us out of the tangle of spiny stems and roots. Sometimes we heard larger stirrings in the dry brush. There were iguanas still close to the settlement. They had been hunted steadily, since they're edible, and some of the men had trained their dogs to track them. The iguanas had learned to scurry into the tangled thickets when they heard anything approaching. They still survived as a memory of the old days on Andros, but they were so poorly adapted to running from dogs and guns that it probably wouldn't be many years before they vanished from the island, as had already happened on the other inhabited Bahamian islands.

Even if there wasn't much place to walk, we went out in the mornings, before the heat became too intense. There was no beach on our north side of the creek, only the headlands, a line of stone about thirty feet above the ocean. The waves hammered away at the hunched cliffs of spongy rock, hollowing out their lower waists. We could scramble down to a few hidden sandy coves, but the current was too strong and the raw edges of the stones too close to us for any swimming. The headlands were weak and honeycombed with pitted stone, leaning over the surging water like someone about to lose their balance, and we always felt uncomfortable standing under their gray weight, with the sea washing tirelessly against our feet.

Since we had no water in our house we had to wash somewhere, even if it was only in salt water. If we crossed the creek we could walk along the dirt road that led to the airstrip; then an overgrown path trailed off from it to the long swath of beach that stretched along the coast south of the creek. Usually there were men in the small ferry boat, and they insisted that we had to know about the dangers in the water. The first time we walked down the bank of the creek to climb into the little boat, holding towels and bathing suits, a man sitting with the boatman began teasing us. He was leaning back against the gunwale, a skinny, hard-muscled man, his dark hands knotted from the same years of hauling in tattered nets and hoisting ragged sails that had scarred Ormond Johnson's hands. His head was covered with a sweat-stained straw hat and his shirt-tail was hanging out of his pants. As he talked to us in a mock serious tone he was slyly looking back at the boatman.

'You go 'long the sand there and it be all beautiful, and the water shiny and clear — but before you know, the shark come. Just like that. One minute you be all alone and then another minute and the shark be there. He goin' to keep you company.'

He couldn't keep himself from laughing at his own description, and his hilarity affected the boatman, who let us drift in mid-stream for a moment as he leaned over his oar to join in the laughter. The two of us were pressed against each other in the center of the boat, with the towels and swimming suits in our laps.

'Big shark,' the boatman went on, still laughing as he

began sculling again, his shoulders and arms heaving in the cork screw motion. 'You don't see him,' a heave of the oar, 'but he be there,' another heave, 'just when you don't want him.'

The two men began laughing uproariously again. The boatman was in one of his cotton shirts that had been washed many times and his khaki trousers that were equally faded. He had torn the sleeves out of all of his shirts to give his arms more freedom as he worked the oar, and most of his pairs of trousers were cut off just above his knees. The muscles of his shoulders were bunched like heavy fists as he sculled against the shining current.

The other man tried to be serious, and he began to tell us about other dangers, but the moment he said the word 'barracuda', the boatman began laughing again. The man finally joined in, taking off his hat and fanning himself with its tattered brim in his exuberant pleasure.

'No, you don't laugh,' he protested finally to the boatman, 'they must know.'

He began again. 'Barracuda, they the ones with the long mouth. Not so big as the sharks, but they be big too. They try to sneak up on you like the shark, but they don't see so good.'

We ground ashore on the ferry landing. With a practised movement the man dropped over the prow of the boat, one hand steadying himself on the gunwale as he dragged the boat's wobbling hull up the ramp after him. He wanted to finish what he had begun to tell us about barracuda.

'They got to come right up close to see you. Then they back off a little and then they come after you. So you got time to be off somewhere.'

'You got time to take a little walk away,' the boatman suggested, laughing even more noisily, and two of them slapped each other on the back. As we picked up our swimming things they grinned and held up their hands to show us they were only partly serious, and we grinned back and started off in the morning heat, a little apprehensive, despite ourselves.

Later, back in the library, when I tried to find out more about the sharks, I was informed that there was a disagreement over how much we had to worry about them. Johann Schopf, who had written about the gritty soil we walked over on our way to the beach, also wrote about the sharks, and he described them as predatory and rapacious:

> . . . the shark is the terror of the Bahama divers and swimmers. The West Indian water, in which such an unspeakable number of fishes live, support these voracious monsters in great plenty. Not less astounding than true are the stories told of what happened during the last war. They say that three days before the battle between Lord Rodney and the Comte de Grasse, whole schools of sharks followed both fleets, and that the sea was so full of them and they crowded so among the islands, that no one dared bathe the least distance from shore. It is probable that the number of corpses from time to time cast overboard from two such large fleets was what tempted these fishes of prey; for in that climate many men died even before the battle, stricken by disease . . .

But another traveler a hundred years later, a Yankee lawyer from New Haven named Ives, wrote, to contradict stories like Schopf's:

> A gentleman who has spent considerable time in the West Indies, assures us that sharks are cautious if not cowardly, and that they will never bite a man if he splashes the water. Perhaps, before trusting too much even to the warm water sharks, it will be prudent to make sure that their hunger has been satisfied. When looking for his breakfast or his dinner, in the absence of

fish, now and then a shark may make a bold dash for human flesh. The very great clearness of the Bahama water may operate in favor of safety, and the fish that they crave for food may be less abundant in the colder water of the Florida gulf. If the Bahama sharks are very dangerous, it is singular that so few facts are reported which indicate it, and that the divers continue to be so numerous and so bold.

It wasn't a dispute we wanted to settle by testing the sharks ourselves. The people in the settlement said little, but they were very cautious about sharks. If we were out in a dinghy and the dark form of a shark glided close, some of them larger than the dinghy itself, no one disturbed them, and there was always a tight watchfulness until the shark was out of sight.

The first sight of the beach always made us catch our breath, no matter how many times we had walked along the rough path before. It was like something you could imagine, but never expect to see. The whiteness of it was blinding, almost iridescent, as if its whiteness had been burnished in the sun. The sand had been rubbed and rubbed until there was nothing left of it but this inexaustible whiteness. It seemed to have no end. It stretched as far south of us as our eyes could see. We could see a faint, dim shape of distant headlands, but we never walked far enough to reach them, even though we often walked for hours.

Sprawling against the slanting lip of white sand was the sea. It was pale and sun-colored close to the shore, then it turned shades of green that ripened into a rich blue that seemed as bottomless as the sky. As we splashed through the ripples of surf the flashing water drops gleamed like flying sparks that left dark patches on our shirts and shorts. We shouted to each other in our excitement as we waded stiff-legged at the edge of the ocean like pale, ungainly water birds that had forgotten how to fly.

We stayed in the shallow water, because what the men in the ferry boat had told us was true. There were sharks in the water, and the surf was so clear that sometimes in the heaving, greenish turmoil as the waves broke close to the shore we could see the long, dark shapes of the prowling fish. Even if we couldn't always see them we could see smaller fish near the surface flashing away desperately as they fled from something larger and menacing in the deeper water. The sharks came so close to the beach that it wasn't possible to swim, except for a nervous dip into the water for a few strokes, one of us taking a turn watching out for the other. Instead of swimming, when we had washed off as best we could, we walked in the glistening sun on the bleached sand, wading down into the water when we saw something curious — sometimes stopping just to look behind us at our wandering footsteps.

If there was enough wind to cool the day a little we went on walking along the endless sweep of the beach, scuffing at the hot sand, trying to run down the gulls who squalled at us as they wheeled up into the gleaming light. We picked up a few of the shining shells, but we left most of them because there were often groups of women from the settlement further along the beach, and they were gathering the shells to earn a little money. The men took the best shells back to Nassau on the sloops, and there was a tourist market for them there. The women idled along in the shallow water, three or four of them together, talking in light, laughing voices, teasing each other and gossiping. They wore their usual faded blouses and wrinkled skirts, with straw hats pulled down over their foreheads and sometimes colored kerchiefs down the back of them to protect their necks. They went bare-legged, and their black skin gleamed like the surface of the shells as they splashed through the long wash of the waves.

The clear golden mornings as we splashed in the surf and

walked along the beach turned into the painful glare of noon if we stayed out too long; so we were usually back in the settlement before the heat was at its worst. There was a stir of activity before lunch — women calling to each other across their gardens, children in ragged shorts running along the edge of the creek, the goats scrambling out of their way. After everyone had eaten the silence fell again. It was time for most people to sleep a little. The tangle of leaves and branches just beyond our window hung in a sighing lassitude that had a heavy, deep breath of its own.

We kept the books we'd brought with us in our suitcases, so usually we read. If Ann was feeling conscientious she studied her German textbooks for her language examination, while I lazily read whatever I could find. Sometimes the books were forgotten and we lay on the creaky iron beds, feeling the slight stir of wind on our skin, our clothes in a messy heap on the bare floor. Then we fell into a light sleep and let the sun slip through the leaves, burning itself out in its sweep through the sky. Even the perpetual buzzing of the insects faded a little in the heat, but a persistent humming sometimes woke us. The windows had no screens and a variety of creatures flapped or glided or buzzed into the openings.

The most troublesome of the insects was a mud dauber wasp that had found the bedroom and was insisting on building a nest somewhere in the shadows. At first it tried to build its small mud structure under the bed frames. But since we kept as persistently knocking off the growing accretions it began instead to carry its small loads of earth to the dangling cord of the light that hung from the ceiling. It was fascinating to watch it work as it swayed on the unsteady cord, wings blurring with its exertions as it patted the sticky mud in place, but we couldn't let it finish. A wasp's nest swinging above our heads could make the bedroom a little crowded.

In the evenings we usually walked to the pier off the side of the church and sat in the darkness, feeling the stirring of the wind, talking into the night. Occasionally the house wasn't empty when we came back to it to sleep. The night insects found their way to it, even if the light wasn't on. Sometimes when we turned on the light switch we would find that one wall of the kitchen was covered with black butterflies each the size of a hand. The sudden glare of light turned them into a wildly fluttering cloud. It was as though someone had torn black paper in pieces, thrown the pieces into the air, and then turned on a fan. We waved our arms and slapped at them with newspapers to drive them out into the darkness. Then as we looked into the corners and along the bare ceiling, searching for any that we might have missed, we could hear the clank of a crab, banging into a floor joist as it lurched its way across the earth beneath us. We slept in the murmured stirring of the wind in the dry shreds of the palms above the house, and the shush of the creek making its way to the sea.

7

Spence

When the first of the recordings we did that summer were released a few months after we left Andros, the telephone began to ring, and we have been getting the same phone calls ever since. Even after so many interviews and all the times we've told the story we still find ourselves being asked again, 'How did you find Spence?'

If we had gone looking for someone like Joseph Spence, I don't think we ever could have found him. Certainly I never heard anyone like him again. Spence was one of the geniuses that sometimes are shaped within a folk music culture, and musicians like him are so unique, and their appearance is so inexplicable, that the people around them simply hold up their hands and don't really try to explain where the talent has come from. Spence, of course, was as modest about his music as all the other musicians we found on Andros. His own perception of his music and his talent was as innocent as everything else about that summer.

But how did we find Spence?

Andros was isolated by the contrary winds and by the poverty of its handful of settlements, but there was considerable travel from settlement to settlement. People sailed into Fresh Creek in small dinghies or in rough handmade boats with a patchwork of sail hugging the bank of the creek, a man hunched over the soaked deck, paddling against the strong current that was trying to sweep the rickety craft out to sea.

There was even a kind of passenger service on coastal sloops that sailed inside the barrier reef, close to the shore, with their decks covered with cages of chickens, live pigs, crates of soft drinks, and building materials of every description. For very little money people could squeeze onto the deck and sail to the next settlement. If the wind wasn't right they'd have to walk back along the beach, but that was accepted as one of the conditions of the life on Andros.

We had gotten to know nearly everyone in Fresh Creek, at least by sight, but often we nodded and smiled at people we didn't know. One afternoon when we were walking through the settlement we came to a group of men who were working on the wall of a new house close to one of the shell-covered paths. Sitting a few feet from them on a pile of bricks was a man playing a guitar. But it sounded too rich for one. After we heard the first few notes I found myself looking behind the wall where the men were working to see where the other guitar player was sitting. There was so much music, such a cascade of notes, that there had to be at least a second guitar playing with him. But there was only Spence. In all the years of recording since then, and with all the guitarists I've worked with, Spence is still in a musical place by himself. He was playing simple popular melodies and hymns, but he was using them as the basis for extended rhythmic and melodic variations. There were sometimes two separate rhythms crossing each other simultaneously, while the melody extended the harmonies into another dimension. He often seemed to be improvising in the bass, the middle strings, and the treble at the same time. Sometimes a variation would strike the men and Spence himself as so exciting that he would simply stop playing, they would forget about their work, and they would shout at each other in their excitement. Finally, one of the men sent a boy from a nearby house to go to the little shop by the boat landing for a bottle of rum, and slowly the others drifted back to work.

Spence talked easily with us, sipping a little rum, calling to friends as they walked past. It was a blazing hot day, and there was a pall of dust from the work on the wall behind us. Spence stayed on his pile of bricks in the shade, a pipe clenched between his teeth, laughing and nodding as we talked. I thought he was about fifty, a large, powerful man in a loose, short-sleeved shirt and khaki trousers. His hair was trimmed short, and his face was still unlined. His fingers were stubbed at the ends, but his hands were strong and quick. He was playing a large, hollow bodied acoustic guitar with a wide fingerboard, so he could finger the complex melodic variations that were central to his unique style. He worked as a stone mason in Nassau, which accounted for the hardened fingers, but there hadn't been any work for several weeks. Many young Bahamian men left the islands to work in the United States on short labor contracts, but an American recession had forced them to return to Nassau and there was serious unemployment. Spence's sister and her husband still lived in Small Hope, a smaller settlement a few miles north of Fresh Creek, so he had come over to stay with them until the job situation improved in Nassau. He had been spending the time seeing friends on the island and playing his guitar for them.

Spence was willing to record for us. He stood up, emptied his bottle of rum, waved goodbye to the men, who were back at work on the wall, and walked with us to our house on the other side of the settlement. On the way we picked up a crowd of older women, one or two of the men, some young girls, and several children. He walked up our wooden steps, put his straw hat on the railing and sat down on the cramped porch on a chair I brought him from the kitchen. The men and women crowded up the steps and leaned against the porch supports. Finally two of them were edged onto the porch with him, almost touching his legs. Ann stayed outside with her camera, I was backed into the kitchen with the tape recorder, the microphone set up outside the door.

Once he'd started, Spence played for nearly an hour, without a break or hesitation. He joked with the girls, they talked back and forth between the pieces, and the older women leaned closer to tease him. I don't remember him ever taking his pipe out of his mouth. His pieces were almost all long instrumental solos, and one of the older women kept asking him to sing. When he protested that he didn't sing she answered, 'What do you mean you don't sing? You got a mouth to talk.'

To please her he did add words to his next piece, the spiritual 'I'm Going To Live That Life', and it was clear that he was at least partly correct in his own estimate of his vocal abilities. He could sing, but the words were mostly unintelligible. He was rhyming against the complex guitar accompaniment, and parts of the text of the piece were worked into his improvisation. It was difficult to understand even occasional words. Somehow, though, this didn't upset the women. His mumbled shouting and the rhythmic freedom of his accompaniment created an excitement that pleased them even more.

Part of the loose swagger of his playing came from the way he tuned the guitar. Spence was playing in a modified standard tuning so he would have more of the guitar's technical resources available for him. The lowest string, which is usually tuned to the note E, was dropped a whole tone to D. With this modified tuning he could make a basic tonic chord, a D chord, with simple fingerings on the top strings. This helped give him more flexibility with his chording, so he could improvise more freely. Usually musicians who improvise extensively work with short phrases and note patterns that they return to again and again. Spence was one of the handful of musicians I've known who could extend an idea through most of a chorus, so that his listeners had to hold their breath to see where the new melodic line would finally lead them. He also conceived each new chorus as a new challenge, and at his most fluid and inventive moments his improvisations developed into a series of variations, rather than the repetition of similar musical ideas that is the usual form other guitarists use for long solos. He was so skilled that he could set a rhythm in a triple meter — 3/4 or 6/8 — against the basic duple meter — 4/4 — of the piece, which is something most improvisers also can do, but Spence was the only one I ever heard who could play both 4/4 — in the lower strings — and 3/4 — in the upper strings — at the same time. With all of his inventiveness he also had an irresistible sense of Caribbean rhythm, so there was a flowing syncopation to everything that he played. Even his early church 'anthems', once he was past the first statement of the melody, took on a Caribbean grace and warmth.

In the hour that he sat playing on the porch with the ring of settlement people shouting and laughing around him, he performed almost every kind of music that was part of the Bahamian folk tradition. It was almost as though he had planned a small concert. He played an extended series of variations on the World War II popular song 'Comin' In On A Wing And A Prayer' that were even more complex and stunning in their rhythmic development than the folk melodies he played. He played anthems, one of them in a 3/4 rhythm. The anthems, with their polyphonic development, sounded almost like music from the seventeenth century. 'I'm Going To Live That Life', was a spiritual, and he was just as excited when he played pieces like 'Brownskin Gal' and 'Jump In The Line', well known 'jump-up' dance melodies that were popular for Nassau parties.

When he felt he had played enough he leaned the guitar against the wall and listened to everything he'd put on the tape, laughing, nodding his head when the music was especially exciting, and exchanging remarks with the people gathered around him. Finally, late in the afternoon, he stood up, still smiling, his pipe still clenched in his teeth, and he and the girls began walking toward the edge of the creek, closer to the ocean. I could hear him playing again as they straggled along the dusty path.

Spence went back to Small Hope on one of the sloops, then we heard he'd traveled back to Nassau, and he was working again as a mason. We didn't see him again on Andros. A few months after our recordings were released Boston Folk musician Fritz Richmond, then producer Paul Rothchild traveled to Nassau to find him, and Pete Seeger called to ask if Spence would be willing to play at the Newport Folk Festival. Until his death in 1996 Spence continued to meet young musicians, some-times traveled to the United States, and he made several more albums. I had released only six of the solos he played on the porch that afternoon on the first album, but after the Boston musicians came to listen to the rest of the pieces I included three others on a collection of Bahamian music that was released four years later. When we met Spence again it was in Boston, in the middle of a cold spring, and for the three of us it was as though we'd come to the end of the world, and there was a familiar face.

Of all the recordings that Spence made, it is those first solos that he improvised on the porch in Fresh Creek that still are the most exciting for me. Sometimes when he was recorded again later he had been working his day job and he hadn't spent as much time with his guitar. The melodies didn't flow as freely. In those weeks he'd stayed with his sister in Small Hope he'd had a chance to practise for hours every day, and when he played for the Fresh Creek people on our porch he was at his most inventive. There was also another difficulty for me with the later recordings. Spence had the island's usual respect for religion, but his family, his sisters and his wife, were deeply religious. They weren't comfortable with his non-Christian music, and someone from the family almost always traveled with him and usually sang on the recordings. In the auditorium in Boston when I sat listening to Spence again, he was mostly playing simple accompaniments as the women sang hymns with him, a serious-faced man wearing a dark suit, a white shirt, and a tie, doing his best to find some way to enliven the simple harmonies of their earnest voices. In the photos Ann took of him later in New York he is flanked by his sister and his wife, who had traveled with him, all three of them staring at the camera with uncomfortable smiles. Spence, for us, would always be the man laughing and joking on our porch, surrounded by the people who understood who he was and what he was playing.

Even if we didn't see Spence again in that summer, he made our lives considerably easier. The guitar was the most popular instrument on Andros, and in every settlement there were young men who played in many different styles. When they heard we had traveled to the island to record folk music they would stop by in the evenings with their guitars to perform for us. There were so many of them, and always in those circumstances there was a question of sensitive feelings; so when they found some place to sit and and there was a crowd around the house where we were staying, I would play them the tape of Spence. If any of them still felt comfortable enough with their own level of ability to stay around to the end of tape, then we would ask them to play. Spence and the sound of his guitar had already become one of the moments that, for us, would always describe the summer.

8

Sharks Again

The young singer who was learning some of the old songs with John Roberts and was going to sing the treble part for the recording had to sail to Nassau, and for a few days John's work on his music came to a stop. When we came by his house he was apologetic, but there was no one else in the settlement who could sing the high notes, and he had to have the third voice. He assured us that '. . . soon August Monday comin''. It was the island's big holiday. At least we had something to look forward to. He nodded his head for emphasis. 'You could hear so much music you listen all day and all night and still you don't hear all of what those boys playin'.'

There were two Andros holidays, Christmas, and August Monday, the first Monday in August, to celebrate the end of slavery in the British colonies. Enough of the summer had drifted past that it wasn't too long to look ahead to August Monday. We had so much to fill the days that we agreed with John that we couldn't think of doing any recording until the other man returned, which could be any time within the next day or the next week, depending on the winds. If we did want to hear some music before then we could listen to the tapes of Joseph Spence.

We also had occasional nights in a small dance pavilion that was still struggling to stay open, even though the workers who had been its reason for being had left. It was simply an enclosed space, open to the sky, with a brightly lit bar at one end and a scattering of tables and chairs around the wooden dance floor. A bulky, light-skinned man named Mr Minnes owned it. He had a round face with a broad forehead and bright, warm eyes. He was young and hopeful, and he always tried to be friendly and cheerful, even though we could see him looking past us at all the other empty tables. We were usually the only customers, but he was always in a neat shirt and his trousers were ironed. The juke box had mostly calypso records, and that summer was the first time we heard The Mighty Sparrow, the king of the calypso singers then, and he is still one of the most important calypso artists today. His light, pleasant voice would fill the brightly lit space with his 'Dear Sparrow', the song we always played as we danced, and to help add a little atmosphere, Mr Minnes would dance with the waitress, who was two or three years younger than Ann. The waitress was slim and pretty, and as gentle as Mr Minnes. Sometimes late at night we could hear them further back along the creek beyond our house. They laughed and talked, and there was a light splashing as they swam together in the creek.

Part of what filled the days in the small wooden house beside the creek was the daily struggle to keep ourselves fed, portioning out the little bit of money we had to get through the summer. We had no problem with water. The water in the creek was too dirty to drink, but there was a water tap not far from the house. The little shed selling provisions across the creek had canned goods with odd and disquieting labels, but we mostly ate the same kinds of things that almost everyone else in the world who lives in a hot climate eats. We ate rice that we bought in thoroughly handled paper sacks at the shed, our neighbors sold us eggs and sometimes vegetables from their gardens — and we ate fish. I didn't know the names of most of the fish we ate. Sometimes people told us what they were, but usually there wasn't anyone around when we had to identify some new variety. The women told Ann which fish were too bony to eat, or which had bad flavor. They warned us that two or three kinds were poisonous, and they described them in careful detail so we would know enough to avoid them. Our final rule of thumb was that if we hadn't been told *not* to eat a certain fish then we went ahead and ate it.

There were, of course, exceptions to this rule. Some of the fish were just too ugly to eat. One afternoon I pulled in a gray shapeless fish about a foot long with a gasping mouth that seemed to be as wide as the fish was long. Its back was covered with long black spines that quivered unpleasantly as it lay heaving on the pier. I was trying to figure out to pull the hook out of the fish's mouth without having to touch it when one of the men passed.

'Him be good fish,' he commented.

'It tastes good?'

'You fry him up. That's good fish.'

Without hesitation I offered the fish to him, explaining that I already had something for our supper. He nodded and with a shrug he knelt down, flipped the hook out of the gaping mouth and lifted the fish up by the tail, all without touching the spines. He nodded his head again and went off down the path, leaving a dripping trail behind him.

Everyone in the village fished, but since most families had a boat of some kind they did their fishing outside the creek. Close to the reef, which was visible as a line of surf a half a mile offshore, there were fish of every size and description. A few days after we'd moved into the little house the Commissioner, as a gesture of friendliness, took us fishing in his large outboard. The settlement's police constable, a large, dark-skinned man with close-trimmed hair who was always smiling, came along to take care of chopping up conch for bait and maneuvering the boat through the shifting currents. We stopped the motor close to the reef and we only had to throw our lines over the side and pull up a string of surprised fish that bit at the piece of conch bait as soon as the hook was dangled in front of them.

When we came back in to shore a few hours later, our arms weary from pulling up the lines and our faces shiny with sunburn, there were enough fish in the bottom of the boat to last us for three or four weeks, but we only took a few of them back to the house with us, despite the Commissioner's generosity, since we didn't have any place to keep them. We finally left the fish in the soft drink cooler of the little shop closest to us, but this was clearly taking advantage of the owner's kindness. He looked at us with a resigned half smile and a half nod when we asked him, a thin, wiry man with a worn and watchful face standing behind his equally worn wooden counter, but his battered cooler, with its dusty bottles of lime soda and cola, was clearly no place for our smelly catch of fish, and we didn't ask him again.

Since we didn't have any way of storing fish, fishing became part of each day's casual rhythm. Ann left it to me, though sometimes she would come down and helpfully stand beside me looking down into the creek and pointing. I have never liked to fish. It always seems to take too much time and too much patience and the catch — at least in Pennsylvania where I grew up — was always too meager to make it worth the effort. Also, I don't like to kill anything, even something that feels as distantly related to me as a fish. But I had to fish, or we wouldn't have anything to eat. So I fished.

Fishing on Andros, however, was different from any of the fishing I'd ever tried before. When the sun slackened its grip on the afternoon I would take a hand-line and some bait and wearing just the summer's khaki shorts and tennis shoes I would walk to the end of the cement pier that was almost directly across the path from the house. The water below it was so clear that I could see down into teeming layers of fish.

They were so hungry that anything I dropped down to them was immediately encircled by picking small mouths.

If you are fishing in water like this — in water that's filled with fish that want to take your hook — you learn to wait for the fish you are particularly hungry to eat. After a few days we had definite ideas about the kinds of fish we liked the best. The rainbow colored turbot were especially delicious, and there were two or three less exotic varieties that were almost as flavorful. The water was filled with small red fish that were coarse flavored and almost too bony to eat and they swarmed after the hook. I had to keep yanking it out of their mouths, playing the line along until something we liked to eat drifted over to see what the other fish were chasing. All I had was a plastic hand-line, but it was much better for fishing like this than a rod would have been, since I could feel the slightest tremor on the line through my fingers. It always felt like I was being nuzzled by an impatient cat.

I didn't have to fish long any afternoon, but I could sometimes have some excitement, even with my small hand-line. One night there was a heavy rain, and the leaves were still bent and shining with dripping streams of water when we woke up. The creek had risen, and when I came down to the pier to fish in the afternoon the water was dark and murky, even though the sun had come out and was beating on me with its usual breathless, golden persistence. I couldn't see below the surface. I baited the hook, threw it in, and after the ordinary spate of small tremors I felt the line catch on something as I was pulling it in. I pulled again and the plastic strained, vibrated with the tension, then parted, somewhere below the surface.

I tried to see down into the current, but, with its brownish burden of silt from the interior of the island, trying to see anything below its glistening surface was almost like looking into a mirror. I tied another hook on the line, cut off another piece of bait, and dropped the line into the stream again. At first there were the same small pickings that I recognized as the hungry teeth of the small, red, bony fish I didn't want to catch, and I jerked the line back and forth, even though I couldn't see what I was doing. Suddenly the line caught again. I pulled at it, trying to free it. There was the same tremor as it strained, and a snap as the line parted.

For a moment I thought about taking the ferry across the creek and buying a can of corned beef for our supper — but a can of anything was too much for our tender budget and I still had some hooks and bait left. I lay down on the pier and tried to look into the water, shading my eyes as I leaned over, but I still couldn't see anything. For a third time I went through the whole process again — tying on a new hook, baiting it with a bit of conch, and then letting it go with a faint splash into the stream. This time, however, when I felt the first tentative nibbles and a sudden grabbing bite I pulled in the line as fast as I could. What I saw was that I had a fish on the hook, but just as it surfaced the water behind it parted and a shark's gray muzzle opened up in a gaping, white semi-circle of teeth that closed on the fish — and at the same time severed my little line again, which I'm sure the shark hadn't even noticed.

I fell back on the pier and gasped. What was a shark doing in the creek? I heard a sudden shouting and saw a ragged gang of children hurrying toward me. They had also seen the shark. They leaned over the pier with noisy excitement.

'He come in because it rain, the water be high,' a ten year old told me seriously, nodding his head as he spoke. Like most of the others he was wearing only a pair of tattered shorts. 'We get him.'

With shrill yelps they rushed off, leaving me on the pier staring apprehensively at the spot only a few feet from me where the shark had disappeared. The commotion had brought Ann out of the house and she was also peering into the current, but she could see as little as I could. I didn't know

what the children had run off for. I think I expected them to
come back with some of the adults. When they did come
back, however, they had brought a length of rope about
twenty yards long, with a great scarred hook bound to one
end of it. Crowding around, two or three of them jumping up
and down in their excitement, they took what was left of my
bait, put it on the hook, and scattered into a circle so there
would be room for the biggest boys to swing the rope. With a
badly coordinated heave that made up in enthusiasm for what
it lacked in strength they managed to fling the hook somewhere into the middle of the stream, and then scampered
back to grab on to the rope.

I didn't know what to be more afraid of — that they
wouldn't catch the shark and it would still be lurking there
when I tried to fish again — or that they would catch the
shark and try to pull it in. From the glimpse I'd had of it the
shark had looked very big. 'Mako shark,' one of the boys had
said. What would happen to them, a gaggle of boys in torn
short pants, if they got a shark on their crude line?

We didn't have to wait long to find out. Catching the shark
was the easiest part of it. In a moment the line sprang taut
and the boys began to shriek with excitement. The surface of
the creek thrashed and heaved, water splashing around us.
Without hesitating they dragged the rope off the pier and
down to the side of the creek so their bare feet could get a
better grip on the mud. For the next few moments there was a
see-saw struggle as the shark tried to tear itself free and they
clung to the rope with a noisy persistence. It was soon obvious that they were the children of fishermen, and that they'd
grown up with fishing lines and sharks. Sometimes one of
them would slip and fall in the mud, and the others would
laugh even more wildly as he scrambled back up, slapping at
his dripping shorts and clutching at the swaying line again.
But at the same time they were inexorably hauling the shark
in toward the shore, maneuvering it toward a place on the

creek bank where there was a low, marshy patch of ground at the edge of the stream.

They were so practised at what they were doing that they soon fell into a semblance of unison in their heaving motions as they pulled the shark closer and closer to them. When its head came out of the water, twisting frantically, they wrenched at the line with even noisier excitement and with all of them dragging at the rope at once they pulled the shark up onto the stretch of mud beside the creek. Out of the water the shark looked huge, and the heavings of it gray, streaming body left deep gouges in the mud.

When the shark's gaspings had become fainter, and it didn't seem possible for it to squirm back into the water the boys began shouting again and they scattered along the paths near their houses. In a moment they were back with sticks and clubs, and slipping up to it cautiously they began to club the shark to death. One boy, we could see, was swinging a much used cricket bat. They were quick to jump out of the way of a flailing jerk of the shark's tail or a heaving gnash of its mouth, but in a moment, between the boys' wild clubbing and its inability to breathe in the air the shark was dead. It was only then that the boys began calling for the adults to come and see what they had done. I still couldn't bring myself to come too close to it, but by a rough measurement I would have said that it was about four boys long — somewhere between fifteen and eighteen feet. It was sharks like this that we glimpsed through the surf when we splashed in the ocean along the beach. Without letting ourselves think about it we walked back to our house. I took some money from our scanty funds, asked the boatman to scull me over the creek and I bought a can of pilchards in the little store. I didn't expect the fish to taste like much, but I had to wait a day or so before I went back to the creek.

Fish, every day, does begin to pall. We got tired of fish.

Everyone else in the settlement, and — we found out later — everyone on Andros — and probably everyone in the Bahamas — was tired of fish. Their answer to this — since fish was what they had to eat — was to make eating fish as much of a taste experience as possible. Small pepper bushes had been planted close to every house, clustered with glistening red pepper pods about the size of a jelly bean candy. When the fish was cleaned the women scored the sides and spread bits of fresh pepper in the scorings. The taste, when the dish was cooked, was all pepper. Somewhere in the midst of the burning sensations was a faint reminder of fish — a suggestion of the texture of fish — but the only thing that your mouth was conscious of was the pepper. Somehow this taste didn't become as monotonous as the taste of fish. For breakfast the fish was sometimes cooked with a heavy brown gravy, but under the taste of the gravy was the familiar tang of pepper.

The electric hotplate in the room we used as a kitchen was primitive, but we were able to cook most things on it. The steady diet of fish, even as strongly peppered as we could manage, became monotonous, but we found many things to try in the strangely marked cans on the grimy shelves in the little shops around the settlement. Some of the stock looked like it might have come from sunken ships, and sometimes the contents tasted like something that had already sunk before the ship went down.

Once, hungering for a sweet dessert to cool our mouths after another meal of peppery fish, we made a special trip across the creek and with some of our precious money we bought a tiny can of condensed milk and a package of raisins. It seemed reasonable that if we added this to the rice and sugar we already had and cooked it all together the result would be rice pudding. The end of the afternoon went into the mixing of all the ingredients in one of our borrowed pans and then a patient stirring as it all boiled together on our hot plate. When we came to ate it, after a turbot I'd caught earlier in the afternoon, we found that it tasted just like all its separate ingredients — like raisins, canned milk, sugar, and rice — without tasting at all like rice pudding.

When you don't have much money, however, and you've spent it on food, you don't throw the food away. You eat it, whatever it tastes like. We sat in the darkened kitchen — we always ate with the lights out to keep our supper a secret from the insects — and slowly picked through the mess on the plates.

'I like the raisins,' Ann said after a moment.

'I think the raisins are pretty good,' I agreed.

The rest of it wouldn't hurt us, no matter what it tasted like. When we finally finished we walked slowly past the yellow, heavy-lidded eyes of the lanterns in the windows of the shadowy houses around us and sat even longer into the night on our pier beside the chapel. It would be time to sleep soon enough.

9

Gal, You Want to Go Back to Scambo

The irrepressible, sweaty swagger of excitement, laughter, music, and exuberant friendliness that was August Monday swept over Fresh Creek like the tide, and sometimes in the distance, late into the night, we could hear the line from the dance song, 'Gal, you want to go back to Scambo', from one of the dance pavilions. One of the singers told us that 'Scambo' means any far away place. For us there couldn't have been any place farther away from the rest of the world than Andros that weekend. We had come to Scambo.

'The Commemoration of the Abolition of Slavery in the British Empire' — the official name for the islands' August Monday celebration — had been noisily under way for three days when the settlement finally struggled to get out of bed and face the morning on Monday. We had already started on Friday night, and John Roberts had been right when he told us, 'you listen all day and all night and you don't hear all what those boys playin' . . .'

The other festivals in the Caribbean have some religious connection or are tied to the yearly rhythms of work. The calypso festival in Trinidad comes at the same time as the Catholic world's Mardi Gras, Barbados' 'Crop Over' Festival comes when the year's sugar crop is in. August Monday just came because that was the date, at the hottest time of the year, and in the middle of what little planting season the islands have. But a celebration is a celebration, and in the

Bahamas it comes the closest to the American Day of Independence. Many Nassau people crowd into the great celebrations at South Hill, south of the city, but many others go back home, which for most of them is a settlement like Fresh Creek on one of the Out Islands.

We could see small boats nudging into the creek all day Friday with families coming back to Andros, and if they didn't live in Fresh Creek they started from the anchorage in the creek to spread out to the smaller settlements like Small Hope, where Spence was living. They were traveling in small motor launches hired for the trip, and they transferred their bags and bundles to smaller sloops and dinghies to get home. A native tour party sailed into the creek on Friday night in a small supply boat. Two men were trading off on the ferry, sculling the heavy boat across from our side of the creek to a construction camp where the holiday crowd was staying. I could see them shaking their heads wearily. Friday night they were up until one a.m., ferrying the crowds back and forth across the creek. On Saturday morning they began again at six a.m.

After the silence and the isolation of our first weeks in Fresh Creek it felt strange to get used to so many people. There was a steady stream of men and women walking past the house on the path beside the creek. Mr Minnes, for once, had people filling the tables at his dance pavilion, and his waitress hurried back and forth with a gleaming smile, rushing to bring everything everybody wanted, since she and Mr Minnes knew that once the weekend was over they would go back to empty tables and occasional visits from the two of us for a carefully measured beer and Mighty Sparrow on the juke box. The people from Nassau were in their holiday best. The men had on ironed trousers and brightly colored shirts, some of them wearing neck ties, all of them wearing new straw hats. Most of the women were in gaudily printed, flowery dresses, though at Mr Minnes's, as they called out to

each other from the rickety tables that were covered with
gaudy paper decorations, some of the younger women had
come in light blouses and tight slacks, their hair done in
elaborate styles that needed a Nassau hairdresser to get right.
Mr Minnes had hung strings of paper lanterns over the dance
floor, and for the night it was jammed with couples dancing
beside us to 'Dear Sparrow'.

The first of the settlement's own dances was held on Friday
night at a hastily erected pavilion, a rough wooden platform,
close to the creek bank. Lights had been strung from poles
across the dance floor and above the glare the palm trees
swayed in the shadows. A small native band played in the
traditional style, with drum, guitar and saw. The drum was
made out of a goat skin tacked over the head of a small, empty
nail barrel, and the drummer had to build a small fire on the
sand and hold the drum over the heat to tighten up the soft
drumhead enough so that the skin made a satisfying thump
when he played it. The band was a loose collection of musicians who happened to be in the settlement that Friday. The
leader was the tall, heavy shouldered, dark-skinned singer
named H. Brown who had improvised the bass part to Roberts'
rhyming at the wake. Mr Minnes's one competitor, the other
local dance pavilion proprietor, had asked Brown to find
somebody to play at his new outdoor dance floor. We had
always thought of Brown as a Fresh Creek native, but he was
from a smaller settlement called Staniard Creek, and he was
only at the creek for the summer. In the economic uncertainties of Andros everyone had to be ready to go where they
could for work. For the dance Brown had put on a new dark
purple shirt with lighter shoulder panels, and he had a red
handkerchief knotted around his neck. He did the band's
singing and he joined in the rhythm with maracas. The guitar
player, a man named Prince Forbes who was wearing a loose
work shirt and dark trousers, was from Mangrove Cay, a
settlement in the southern half of Andros. He worked on one

of the small sloops, and they had been trying to sail to Nassau when the wind had died and left them slack sailed on the water in the summer's dazzling heat. After a day of dead calm the sloop had finally drifted into Fresh Creek with the tide that afternoon.

When I met Forbes at the dance and I heard he was from the south I asked him about McQueen. Did he know anything about him? Forbes and the other men from his boat nodded. McQueen was sailing on a fast sloop called the Charity, and he was living in a settlement called Lisbon Creek, about seven miles from their settlement at Mangrove Cay. I asked them if McQueen was still singing, and there was an embarrassed silence. One of them finally said uncomfortably that McQueen spent most of his time drinking rum, and his voice wasn't strong the way it used to be. One of the others protested.

'McQueen's still the best there is, for his style of singing.'

'Only if he don't be drinkin'.' Prince Forbes insisted. 'But that's right. He still the best there is.'

The men scattered off into the settlement, leaving Forbes with his guitar on the dance pavilion's rickety steps.

When the band tentatively picked its way into its first song, we could see that another man, wiry muscled, serious-faced, was playing a saw. Nearly everywhere in the islands — from the Bahamas to the Caribbean islands to the south — the little pick-up bands use some kind of rasp to emphasize the dance rhythms. In the Cuban bands there are elaborate hollow gourds with one side scored to leave a set of ridges on the gourd's hard surface. The gourds are painted with the same colorful designs as the maracas, and they are played with a stick that the player drags across the scored ridges. There was no gourd to play in the Fresh Creek band, so the man was using an ordinary carpenter's saw, scraping a table knife back and forth over the saw's teeth. He held the saw with the handle against his left shoulder, the blade in his left hand.

His right hand, with the table knife, kept the rhythm. The sound was like the metallic rubbing of the 'frottoir', the ridged sheet of metal that is an essential part of the sound of a Louisiana zydeco band. He was going to spend most of Tuesday with a file sharpening the saw again, but in the enthusiasm of the dance, as he swayed with the rhythm under the sagging strings of lights, Tuesday seemed a long way off.

'Gal, you want to go back to Scambo'. Everybody liked the song, so Brown sang it three or four times during the dance. There wasn't any kind of microphone, but his voice was still warm and loudly cheerful late into the night. Prince Forbes was playing a small acoustic guitar; so Brown didn't have to sing too loudly to be heard over the rest of the ragged band. He didn't care if we recorded the music, and when we first listened back to the tapes we were startled to hear a persistent wooden clicking that surrounded the rhythm. The children from the settlement, wearing their best T-shirts and shorts, were so much part of the night's inexhaustible enthusiasm we had forgotten that they ringed the band, tapping out the rhythm on sticks. So many people had crowded onto the dance floor and onto the little stretch of beach around it that we often couldn't see the band. Most of the Nassau people were too busy to dance, talking to old friends, or drinking, but there was a glow of excitement that hung over the wavering lights. In their faces I could see that they had come back to Scambo.

Saturday took a few hours to begin again, since there were hangovers to deal with and old friends who still hadn't been visited. But by the evening the mood had picked up. That night we couldn't get everywhere to hear all of the music. A commercial calypso band, with music from Trinidad and the rest of the Caribbean but almost nothing from the Bahamas, came over in the supply boat and set up their instruments in a dance pavilion in the old construction camp behind the hotel on the other side of the creek. H. Brown was back at the dance floor by the creek, still singing, his voice still friendly and still ringing out into the shadows. Before they could begin, the drummer had lit his fire again to tighten the primitive drum head and the smell of the fire still hung over the dangling lights.

We all rested on Sunday. The newcomers visited their families. Chickens were boiled, pepper was strewn into fish stews. The settlement was a mosaic of voices, laughter, and barking dogs. Early on Monday morning a small sloop came slowly into the anchorage inside the mouth of the creek, the deck crowded with men. We were sitting on our porch and someone walking by called out that the boat was from Cargill Creek, one of the small settlements south of Fresh Creek. Usually the sloops pulled a dinghy behind them so the crew could get in closer to shore, and as we sat watching, the men pulled the dinghy up to the side of the boat, bailed it out, then one of them carefully leaned down and propped a large bass drum between the boards. The bass drum was sculled to shore; then the rest of the men climbed into the dinghy, carrying a snare drum and three trumpet cases. It was the brass band from Cargill Creek. They had been hired to play at the other dance pavilion on our side of the creek.

John Roberts and the other older people in the settlement had told us about the brass bands when we asked them about Andros music. The bands were another element of the Andros musical tradition that the natives had inherited from the British. We knew that there were three of the bands on Andros. One at Staniard Creek, this one from Cargill Creek, and the third from the settlement of Mangrove Cay, south of the bights that split Andros in two. The Staniard Creek band sometimes had a saxophone, and there had been someone who

played the melophone in the Mangrove Cay band for a number of years, but the usual instrumentation was trumpets and drums. We had been impatient to hear the music of the bands, but John assured us there would be brass bands at the dances. When he had told us that on August Monday there would be more music than we could listen to, he added that 'one, maybe two' of the bands would be there playing somewhere.

We walked toward the pavilion, listening for the sound of trumpets. The musicians weren't professionals. They were fisherman and they farmed small garden plots, and they picked up their instruments when there was a job to play and they left them in their cases most of the time when they didn't have a job. They were pressed into service for dances on the holidays, but their commonest jobs were funerals. They led the procession carrying the coffin from the church to the cemetery. We could hear them beginning to warm up in a small shed beside the pavilion, and they sounded just like they should have sounded, like fishermen who didn't have much time to practise their instruments, but there was a warm vocal style to their playing, and it was clear that they loved these moments when they could make music together.

The leader of the band was a middle-aged man named Kingston Brown. He was very guarded, thin; a dark-skinned man who looked us over very carefully before he stopped to talk to me. He was wearing freshly pressed white flannel trousers, a light suit jacket, and a new straw hat. As we talked I kept wondering how he could have sailed most of the night in a small sloop with seven other men and kept his white trousers neatly pressed and out of the way in the cramped cabin space under the deck. The band had brought along three trumpets, but the third instrument stayed in its case. It belonged to a third member who was the local police constable at another settlement in the south, and he had to stay behind to be sure that his local celebration didn't get too excited. The band had brought his trumpet along in case one of theirs developed valve trouble. The bass drum they had ferried ashore in the dinghy was lettered 'St Bartholomew's Friendly Society', and the drummer assured me that they were the society's official band. The society was a fraternal order that had occasional meetings in the settlements along the Andros coast, and one of their jobs was to play for the procession that opened the meeting.

Kingston hesitated when we asked him about recording. He looked back across the creek, he looked up into the palm trees. The rest of the band was excited at the idea. There was a noisy discussion. Kingston was worried about the dance job they had been hired to play. They were supposed to play for the dancers for eight hours, and he thought it would be better if they rested first. Eight hours on a dance job would be a long trial even for dance band professionals, and his band was all-amateur. But his opposition was half-hearted. He'd never heard how the band sounded. He talked to the others again, people from the settlement crowding around to be part of the conversation, and finally his curiosity got the better of him. Two of the boys from the settlement picked up the drums and we trailed after them along the paths to our house. As we picked our way over the paths' rough stones and crushed shells most of the people from the settlement came out of their houses to listen.

Kingston was so worried about his musicians' endurance that there was no time for more than a rough tuning. They grouped themselves around the microphone, and at a signal from Kingston, nodding with his trumpet to his lips, they slowly, breathily, and earnestly played a hymn with the kind of four-square harmonies and sturdy rhythm that are typical of Salvation Army brass bands. People around us laughed and cheered. The band had only time to perform two more short hymns, as stately and half-tuned as the first, and then Kingston waved his hands. That was all they would do. They had to save their lips for the job. He stood listening back to the tape with the first smile I'd seen from him, and in a moment the trumpets were back in their cases and the boys from the settlement were scurrying back across the clearing in front of the house with the drums.

The settlement stayed up late into the night. Even if we'd wanted to sleep, there was too much noise and too much excitement. The raw smell of rum hung over everything, and in the dark we could hear people crashing through the bushes as they lost their way and walked off the meandering paths into the shadows. The calypso band was playing across the creek, H. Brown was playing with his little jump-up band at the new band stand, the brass band was at the other pavilion, Mr Minnes was playing his juke box as loud as it would go, and in every little store in the settlement there was someone with a guitar.

We could hear that the St Bartholemew's Friendly Society brass band was sounding badly frayed, but they had added enough volunteer drummers and rattle players out at the edge of the lights to make up for the fading trumpet players. Kingston finally began to sing every piece he could remember the words to, and when he ran out of those he started to make up words. Along the creek we could hear H. Brown singing again, 'Gal, you want to go back to Scambo'. He still had some voice left, though he probably wouldn't be able to talk much the next day.

Kingston Brown and his band was the last to stop playing. At two a.m. the weak sound of the last trumpet faded into a breathy gasp, then the sounds of singing and laughing slowly died. When we walked back to our house we could hear people on both sides of the creek shouting to the ferry men to hurry across with the boat. One of the scullers had gotten as drunk as his passengers, and he was sprawled out in the back of his boat, letting volunteers scull it across for him. On the other side of the creek the ferry man was trying to tie his boat up to the dock. A woman was arguing with him.

'What do you mean you aren't going to take me across?'

'I know your face. I taken you across several times tonight.'

'But I must sleep over there.'

The ferry man stood in the shadows looking at her, his back bent and his shoulders slumped. Finally he shrugged.

'I should leave you here.'

He wearily untied the boat and began sculling her across the creek's murmuring current. The last sounds of August Monday were the creak of his oar and the sound of her voice singing softly in the stillness.

10

A Walk On The Beach

The summer was slipping past, but once the excitement of August Monday had stormed out of our lives we went back to our quiet days of walking in the sun, swimming very carefully a few yards off the beach as we watched for sharks, and sitting in the darkness on the pier beside the chapel, talking late into the night. Ann was studying for her language exam again, and her notes for German grammar and vocabulary collected on our kitchen table. I fished every day off the little pier in the creek. In the mornings I listened to the tapes we'd recorded and made notes on what the musicians had told us. We didn't know what would happen to us at the end of the summer, and for these last few weeks, the small house was still the only place we had to live. We would have to decide what we were going to do sometime, but for a few more weeks things went on as they had before, even if the sun hung a little heavier in the sky and the bushes along the path to the beach had burned drier and dustier with the summer's passage.

On the Sunday after the August Monday celebration John Roberts finally came to the house with his two singers. H. Brown had gotten his voice back after the weekend of singing with the little band. Charles Wallace, a slim, light-skinned man who was anxious to do whatever he felt we wanted, had finally come back from Nassau, and he and Brown had learned enough of John's old songs so they could join in with him on the recording. As we were testing the microphone Brown and

Wallace sang a gospel duet for us, and what they liked to perform themselves was the kind of gospel quartet music that they heard over the radio. It was the current American gospel music style, which for them made it even more tempting. Part of John's awkward modesty was the fact that he couldn't sing that way, and he was certain that his old kind of songs would soon die out because most of the young people didn't want to know about them.

In our kitchen, with the three men hunched around the microphone, hands cupping one ear as they sang, we finally heard 'Dig My Grave'. We had come so far and I had waited so long to hear it, that the moment passed almost as an anticlimax. John cupped his hand to his ear, nodded to the other two and began singing.

> Dig my grave so long and narrow,
> Make my coffin so neat and strong.
> Dig my grave so long and narrow,
> Make my coffin so neat and strong.
>
> But two, two to my head,
> Two, two to my feet;
> But two, two to carry me,
> Whenever I die.
>
> Oh Lord, my soul's going to shine like a star,
> My little soul's going to shine like a star,
> Lord my little soul's going to shine like a star,
> Oh, on Mount Calvary.

He had taught them the traditional way of singing the song, with their voices following his in counterpoint. When he sang 'Two, two to my head . . .' they followed him a few beats later, like a round. John himself might have felt self-conscious about his old way of singing, but I was aware as we sat crowded together in the heat and the close stillness of the little kitchen that they respected him and his place in their tradition in ways that John could not really understand. I was conscious that at this moment, when John was giving so much of his music to Ann and to me, he was also passing on something that was just as important to the two younger men.

The song was as moving, as unique, as individual as I had dreamed it would be. There is no other song like it in the Bahamian tradition, and even though I spent hours in library files that year trying to find a source for it somewhere else, it still seems to be unknown anywhere but in the islands. It was included in the earliest Bahamian song collections. Who was the unknown singer who had written it? The song was so simple, but it opened so many doors for me. It cast a light on the past of this small African group that had been left on this forgotten island, and forced to assimilate another culture. They, in their turn, had brought to the new culture a sensitivity and responsiveness that remade everything they touched and heard. 'Dig My Grave' was the touchstone for so much else I heard in the many years of listening to African-American music that were to come after.

John had taught them other hymns and anthems. After 'Dig My Grave' they sang a simple hymn 'Depend on Me':

> Oh 'pend on me, I will 'pend on you,
> Faithful servant, I want to be:
> When you hear my trumpet sound then —
> But you can depend on me.

As they repeated the verses John began to slip into the free rhythms of the rhyming style, but he drew back and they ended with a simple chord before he had begun to expand the text more fully. It was on the next hymn, 'Take Your Burden To The Lord And Leave It There', that suddenly John broke free from the rhythm and began rhyming. The other two voices were the anchor that he pulled against, but his inten-

sity lifted them with him and their harmonies began to shift
rhythmically. It was that same moment of collective improvisation we had heard at the wake. The thin wooden walls of the
kitchen shook with the strength of the singing.

> Leave it there, Lord, leave it there,
> Take your burden to the Lord and leave it there;
> If you trust and believe He will surely treat you right,
> Take your burden to the Lord and leave it there.

John had a harsh, rough, voice, almost as deep in range as H.
Brown, who was singing the bass harmonies, and the deep
tones seemed to burn into the walls of the kitchen. Wherever
he had come in his improvised text John would hold a note at
the end of each verse, sustaining it until the bass and the
treble picked up the harmonies of the next stanza. The note's
tone was hard and insistent. He was compelling the other two
to follow his voice. The rhythms were a complex overlay
against the basic structure of the hymn — but we could still
tap our feet to the pulse of the singing. It was this layering
that I learned later is the shadow of Africa in the music of its
scattered peoples. The rhythmic stress is delayed, the harmonies are modified. Just as we had experienced with Joseph
Spence's guitar solos we were hearing a complex interweave of
culture and memory. What we were immediately conscious
of, however, was that we were experiencing some of the most
exciting singing we had ever heard.

John had also taught the other two singers the chorus
melodies for the classic Andros ballads. We didn't know,
until that moment, that singers like McQueen and Roberts
were not only rhymers. They had created a whole ballad
tradition built on their lives as fishermen and sailors in the
isolation of Andros. The ballads were long, complicated nar-
ratives of sailing journeys that had ended tragically, of
drownings, of ships trying to cross to Andros, of the failed
attempts to establish businesses on the island. Just as on the

other islands scattered around the Caribbean, the Bahamian song tradition grew out of the harsh reality that most people on islands like Andros couldn't read or write. If they wanted to create their own histories and traditions then they would have to sing them, or find some other way to remember them. Again, as we had felt so often before, Andros had opened a window for us. A window opening to the way a culture — the way a group of people live together and share their lives — grows and learns and is created and renewed.

What H. Brown and Charles Wallace learned were responses to the stories John sang. The responses were like the kind of one-line choruses that you can hear in a traditional Scottish pub, where the old ballads are still heard.

In the ballad of the ship Pytoria that sank in a storm, John began:

In nineteen hundred and twenty-nine ,

and they responded:

Run come seek, Run come seek.

The second line of the verse was a repeat of the first:

In nineteen hundred and twenty-nine,

but they resolved the verse harmonically with:

Run come seek it, Jerusalem.

The ballad was a detailed, moving description of the sinking of the Pytoria and the drowning of the thirty-four 'souls' on board, all within the musical framework of John's narrative singing and their surging responses. We had begun our journey to hear a simple hymn, and now we were hearing so much else.

In nineteen hundred and twenty-nine,
    Run come seek, run come seek,

In nineteen hundred and twenty-nine,
   Run come seek it, Jerusalem.

There was three sails leaving out the harbor,
   Run come seek, run come seek,
There was three sails leaving out the harbor,
   Run come seek it, Jerusalem. . .

Will you name those three sails for me,
   Run come seek, run come seek,
Will you name those three sails for me,
   Run come seek it, Jerusalem.

The Result, The Myrtle, The Pytoria,
   Run come seek, run come seek,
The Result, The Myrtle, The Pytoria,
   Run come seek it, Jerusalem. . .

Now the first sea hit the Pytoria,
   Run come seek, run come seek,
Thank God, everybody get confused,
   Run come seek it, Jerusalem.

Now the second sea hit the Pytoria,
   Run come seek, run come seek,
Now she knock little Era to Glory,
   Run come seek it, Jerusalem.

Now she had thirty-four souls 'board her,
   Run come seek, run come seek,
Now she had thirty-four souls 'board her,
   Run come seek it, Jerusalem. . .

It was typical of John, serious and shy, to be uncomfortable
with the recordings when he came to the house two days later

to listen to what they had done on Sunday. He was also going to record a new song for us. He wouldn't sing a boat launching song for us on the first day because it was a Sunday, and the launching song was slightly suggestive. The launching songs were also part of the Andros tradition. The recordings that I had heard in the University of California library and that had brought us to Andros had included a launching song. Alan Lomax, who had made the recording, described the people in one of the settlements singing the song as they pulled on the lines to draw a sloop from the beach into the sea, so pleased with their singing that they kept it up until the water was up to their necks.

At many of the settlements the men still built their own sloops. The keel was laid on a roughly constructed frame on the beach, and when the boat was finished the whole settlement came to help put the new sloop in the water. The singing helped coordinate the rhythm of the hauling, just like the work chanties on old sea-going sailing vessels had helped keep the crew together when they hauled on the sail lines or the anchor chain. The lead singer at an Andros launching kept everybody pulling together. At the same time he was expected to improvise new verses for the song, praising the captain who had built the boat and greeting new people who had come down to the beach to help pull on the lines.

There was no boat-building at Fresh Creek but John described the launchings he had sung for at other settlements when he was growing up.

'Now you see a crowd of people get around the boat, you understand, and they have ropes rig out to launch the boat, the boat up on the beach. And they launch the boat and they pull and they sing. As they pull they sing.'

I asked him if everybody in the settlement came out and he nodded emphatically.

'Oh yes, everybody. That's the rule up here. Any boat can

be launched what's new built; everybody goes there to launch her, to put her in the water.'

John's launching song was simple and short, and he sang it sitting in the same chair in our little kitchen where he had sat when he recorded 'Dig My Grave' two days earlier. Even for someone who was deeply religious, as John was, the launching song didn't seem to be offensive, but he would only sing it on some other day of the week. His launching song was about the girls of the settlement pulling on the lines.

Young gal, go swing your tail, swing your tail
    to the southwest gale,
Young gal, go swing your tail, swing your tail
    to the northwest gale.

Everybody gather 'round,
    Young gal, go swing your tail,
Everybody get 'round this boat,
    Young gal, go swing your tail.

Boys and girls get troubled in mind,
    Young gal, go swing your tail,
Boys and girls get troubled in mind,
    Young gal, go swing your tail.

Everybody get converted,
    Young gal, go swing your tail,
Everybody get converted,
    Young gal, go swing your tail. . .

'See it's short, you know. That's all of that in that launching. At the last, that time, you say "Young, gal, go swing your tail," they pull. And then she goes.'

He stayed for another hour in the kitchen, listening again to the music he had recorded. We could feel him struggle with his pleasure at hearing what he and the other two had done, and his own innate, gentle modesty. After we talked for a few more minutes, and he told us the story of some of the songs, it was his modesty that won out. He shook his head ruefully.

'That ain't right.'

He knew, and we knew, that he had performed movingly for us there in the little kitchen with the two young men he had taught his songs, but he couldn't bring himself to say that he was the singer we had come to find. He stood up from his chair and shook his head again.

'You got to see Frederick McQueen.'

So much of the summer had passed, and we had learned so much and heard so much that we decided to do what John told us. It was time to search for Frederick McQueen. We knew now that the place to look for him was on the south of the island, below the bights in a settlement called Mangrove Cay. I checked with the schedule of the mail boat, and it would be anchoring off the creek mouth in four days. It would take us to the last settlement before the bights, and we would try to find a sloop to take us further on. We didn't have a lot to pack, since we hadn't accumulated much except a few sea shells and the notes and the tapes from the recordings. Our neighbors were still in the summer languors that followed August Monday.

One afternoon when we were walking by the landing at the end of the creek we saw that one of the small sloops that took freight on its deck was loading up, and it was about to sail to Small Hope, the next settlement about fourteen miles north along the beach. On an impulse I said to Ann that we'd never been on one of the sloops — why didn't we sail with them? She hesitated, but I was so swept up into the idea of sailing along the coast, and I was so persistent that she let herself be talked into it. There was a three-man crew on the boat; a blocky, round-faced man in a torn white shirt who was in charge of the loading and the steering, and two weary, thin, smaller men who handled the sails and carried everything from the wharf up onto the cramped deck. For a few dollars they made a place for us between the cases of soft drink bottles and a large, trussed pig that was noisily and unhappily stretched across the weathered deck in front of the small cockpit.

When the two crewmen hoisted the ragged sails the stained canvas filled with a soft, steady wind, and the sloop glided out of the anchorage and into the open water between the headlands and the reef. There was no feeling of movement. It was as though we had stretched out wings and we were gliding like the gulls that had gathered from the creek to follow us. It was a moment of complete peacefulness. Even the pig seemed to feel the mood, and after another minute of futile squirming against its bindings it fell asleep.

The shore slipped past, the shadows of the headlands giving away to an unbroken stretch of beach that was as white and as unmarred as the beach where we swam south of the creek. About half way there was a tremor as the sloop lumbered through the current of another large creek that broke through the beach and emptied into the ocean. The clumsiness of the primitive boat gave it its steadiness when the winds were right and the water was as smooth as this edge of coastline between the beach and the reef. The sunset cast long, golden shadows across the surf toward us.

There was a ragged wharf at Small Hope, and the sloop stayed long enough only to unload and continue on toward the north. We stood in the silence and watched the sails fill again with the calm breath of the wind. I had thought optimistically that we could find some kind of boat that was sailing back to Fresh Creek, or that there might be someplace to stay in Small Hope, but when we walked into the settlement and looked at the handful of houses, as poor and as weather-beaten as the ones in Fresh Creek, and then turned again to look at the empty anchorage, we realized that we were going to have to walk the fourteen miles back. The late afternoon was calm enough, and the sky was clear enough that the walk didn't dismay us. We'd be back in time to go to Mr Minnes's for a beer and Mighty Sparrow on the juke box.

After our weeks on the island we were both tanned and thin, and we had spent so much time walking that we were used to the beaches. But I hadn't thought enough about what we were doing. I had been too impulsive. Fourteen miles is a long way to walk on beach sand, even a beach swept with waves so that some of the sand is hard packed. I hadn't thought about anything to eat or drink. I had thought we could find something in Small Hope, but there was nothing there. Ann looked at me, waiting, and I shrugged with what I hoped was casual confidence, and we began walking along the beach. There would never be another summer when I would be so innocent.

Among the other things we didn't have with us were flash lights. We were so used to the paths of Fresh Creek that we didn't need any light when we walked in the dark to the wharf by the chapel or to Mr Minnes's bar. As the sun became entangled in the trees and the brush to the right of us, sinking over the still center of the island, we had to walk slower, more carefully. Our eyes could still pick up the line of the surf, but the darkness was a muffling presence that crowded out everything else.

Was Andros haunted? We had been told so many stories about the spirits that haunted the island. About the small spirit called the 'chickcharnie' that tied the tops of three trees together, and in the darkness you could see its red eyes staring at you. About the more dangerous spirits that lived in the large rotten apples that grew in the swamps in the center of the island. You could stay away from the spirits by avoiding the smell of the apples. About birds that were the contacts for the spirits, and you could tell they weren't real because their eyes closed from side to side, not up and down like human eyes. Whatever we had thought about the spirits before, they suddenly were part of the tumult of sensations that we felt around us in the growing dusk.

We couldn't say today if we thought Andros was haunted, but it was a long night on that dark beach, and many things happened. A few miles south of Small Hope the beach narrowed and, as we kept walking, we had to edge closer and closer to the darker smudge of shadows in the brush. Finally, looking for some kind of path to follow, we tried to walk away from the beach into the thicket. There was a whine of mosquitoes as they rose around us, but there was something else. Our faces felt buffeted, as if something was insistently slapping at our cheeks. Not hard, just a steady, persistent slapping. After a few steps we retreated back to the beach and splashed through the shallow surf until the beach widened out again.

The wind suddenly became heavier, and there was the first splattering of rain. We had talked a little at the beginning of the walk, but now we trudged on silently, heads down, trying to keep from stumbling over things that had washed up on the beach. By the time we reached the creek that emptied into the sea half way to Fresh Creek the rain was streaming down, the wind was buffeting the trees behind us, and close to the shore there were blinding flashes of lightning knifing down into the water. In the momentary, eerie glare we could see the gray, tossing surface of the sea and the streaming current of the creek between us and the beach that led south. It was too far to go back to Small Hope, and there was no shelter of any kind where we were.

When I had asked the men on the sloop about the walk back along the beach they had warned me seriously about crossing the stream. We shouldn't walk right out into the

water, and cross straight to the other side. There was quick
sand close to the shore.

'You can't see it when you walkin', but it be there.'

We would have to walk out into the ocean and circle back
to the shore. They had also told us that the mouth of the
stream was a place where sharks lingered.

'They come there so you walk fast. They be waitin' where
the creek come into the sea.'

We stood in the darkness with the wind swirling around
us, the rain washing down our faces, the lightning flashes
showing us only gray tossing stretches of water. There was no
way to know how deep it would be or what we would step
into once we'd started across. The situation I had gotten us
into was so foolish that we wouldn't have known how to talk
about it, even if we could have heard each other over the roar
of the wind and the surf. I waded slowly into the water, trying
to feel the bottom with my feet, and Ann followed, reaching
forward to hold on to the back of my belt. The water rose
around us, coming in surges from the sea and beating against
the rushing current of the stream. I could feel the sand
growing softer and softer under us, then I stumbled into some
kind of pit gouged into the bottom and we had to throw
ourselves forward, half swimming, half pulling at the water
with our arms as we struggled through it. There was another
flash of lightning and we could see that we were further out
from the shore than we had wanted to be and the under-
current of the sea was pulling at our legs. Ann's hand was still
holding on to the back of my belt. After another wrench
forward I suddenly felt firmer sand under my feet. Another
ten yards in the darkness and the water had dropped to our
waists. We were across.

After a few more miles the rain stopped, and the clouds lifted
enough that we could see the white scud of the surf up the

beach. The sand was firmer after the flooding and we could walk more quickly. We held hands, tired, hungry, thirsty, but certain that we'd find our way back to Fresh Creek. A mile north of the first houses the beach ended against the headlands. There was a path through the brush that led to the back of the settlement. We began to walk more quickly, ready to strip off our soaked, salt-stiffened clothes. Then at a turning of the path we suddenly stopped. Ahead of us we both saw the tops of three trees twisted together and red eyes looking down at us. We held our breath and after a moment we lowered our heads and hurried even more quickly over the rough path.

When we finally were in dry clothes and we had finished some food that we had left from lunch there still was time for Mr Minnes, whose smile was confused but friendly as he saw us come in so late. We were again his only customers. We were too tired and stiff to talk, but we could dance, a last time to 'Dear Sparrow', as Mr Minnes and his pretty young waitress danced beside us.

11

The Pleasures of Sailing

The mail boat was going to take us south to a settlement called Behring Point, but we still had a day and a half to wait after our night walk on the beach from Small Hope. We went to our neighbors and thanked them for their help. We returned the pans we had borrowed from the Commissioner. The woman who had rented us the house showed as little expression as she had when we'd moved into the house, but she waved her pipe with what seemed to be a friendly gesture of goodbye. By this time most of the people in the settlement knew we were going to go to the south of Andros to try to find Frederick McQueen. Voices called out after us.

'You goin' find him. You see. McQueen be down there somewhere.'

On the day we were to leave the winds were stronger than anything we'd experienced before. The sky was gray and barred with darker banks of cloud. We had heard from one of the men by the pier that there was a hurricane warning on the radio. The mail boat that was going to take us to the settlement of Behring Point didn't reach Fresh Creek until about two in the afternoon. It came inside the break in the reef and stood off while a small skiff that the crew winched off the deck came in to the shore. It was a small, battered coastal steamer, with two cramped decks for passengers, the mail, and whatever supplies they could take along with them. When the skiff came into the pier the two crewmen in it said that the anchor cables had dragged the night before, and the winds had nearly driven the ship onto the rocks at Mastik Point. By this time the sea was heaving in the driving wind. We lowered our bags and suitcase and the tape recorder from the pier into the swaying skiff and clambered down hesitantly beside the two men who were holding up their arms to help us.

As the small skiff edged close to the ship the crewman at the rudder struggled to steer the small boat against the side of the heaving ship. His hands were knotted tensely around the worn rudder pole. We were pitching so wildly that I couldn't see how we could get on board. The waves were cresting in swells several feet high and the men in the skiff had to pass our things one piece at a time onto the deck, waiting for the swell to lift the skiff out of the troughs of the waves. When the deck of the skiff rose unsteadily to the height of the ship the bags and the tape recorder were handed to men leaning over the side of the ship. Then we had to scramble on board as best we could. We didn't have time to think about what we were doing. The men in the careening skiff pointed to rusty cables trailing down the ship's side, and when the swell lifted us again we pulled ourselves onto the deck as best we could, clinging to the cables. The moment the grinding winch had lifted the skiff onto the deck the ship slipped through the break in the reef to get to the open sea.

When we were beyond the reef there was an unmistakable sense of relief on the ship. The crew could handle the ship on the open water. We were still sitting on the deck, holding on to the tape recorder and our bags to keep them from sliding into the gunwales. We could see that the ship was old, but the company was trying to keep it in condition for the weekly runs. The decks and the bulkheads were pitted with rust, but there had been some effort to keep the metal painted. The deck was scarred and worn, but it had been cleaned sometime earlier in the day. Despite the swell, when we had cleared the reef most of the crew went to their hammocks to try to get some rest. They had had little sleep the night before. As the ship steered into its course to the south we could see a man in a flapping shirt and trousers at a railing in the stern dragging a heavy fishing line in the ship's wake. Just outside the reef a large barracuda took the bait and he yanked it up onto the deck, the fish flapping desperately with flashing jaws a few feet from us. As it twisted across the deck the man struck at it with a hammer until it was finally still.

About sunset, with the wind dropping, the ship reached the anchorage off Behring Point. We could see a small cluster of houses on a low rise above the beach. The settlement was the farthest south that the ship would take us. At Behring Point the coast rounded away toward the interior of the island. The settlement had been built at the point where North Bight flowed into the ocean, and the bight, the first of the three broad, gleaming sweeps of water that divide Andros into the northern and southern halves, stretched beyond us toward the hazy shoreline dimly visible through the low clouds to the south. The water was still so rough that the skiff drove onto the rocks a few yards offshore, but people from the settlement were waiting on a small stone pier, and they pulled our luggage and the tape recorder and the ship's freight out of the skiff and took us back toward the houses on the rise above the beach. We could see that there was a denser growth of trees at Behring Point than at Fresh Creek, and we found ourselves standing in a green swath of shade as we waited for the local constable to come for us. The clouds were breaking up, and there were already streaks of sunlight slanting through the leaves.

The constable was David Mackey, the third trumpeter from the St Bartholomew's Friendly Society band. He was the band member who had to stay in his own settlement to keep things peaceable on August Monday, and it was his trumpet that the band had brought with them in case they had valve trouble. The band had told Mackey about us when they'd sailed back to the south, and he was waiting for us to reach his settlement. He was a strong-looking, middle-aged, dark-skinned man with some of the warm affability of Joseph Spence. He was older, his face was lined, and his eyes were watchful, but he was always ready to smile. He didn't wear a uniform, though he had one for formal occasions. His stucco house, at the top of the slope in a thick growth of trees and a careful garden, overlooked the scattered houses of the small settlement. The house was old-fashioned, and it didn't have electricity, but it was a big house, and he insisted that we stay in one of his rooms for the night.

His wife told us that his son had just been there a moment before with his family, and David went to the porch and called his son's name. Fifty yards away through the trees we could see a tall, thin young man turn, hand a baby wrapped in a blanket to his wife walking beside him, and come running back to the house. In a moment he was standing in front of his father, smiling affectionately at him, and saying as he stopped, 'Sir?'

Mackey had his wife kill a chicken for us for dinner and we sat in the shadowy living-room, crowded with old-fashioned furniture and book shelves and pictures that loomed over us from the walls, as he talked about the difficult and unsatisfactory political situation in the islands until supper was ready. We ate in a small dining room by kerosene lamp. Supper was the chicken, hand ground corn grits, and cocoa. We had been told by several of the men who had worked in the United States that they couldn't get used to the chicken they were served in America. It was soft like mush. There was nothing to get their teeth into. This chicken had spent its short life scrabbling in the garden and running from the assorted creatures, wild and tame, that pursued it. We could get our teeth into it, but we could barely chew it, despite the rich flavor of David's wife's cooking.

During the dinner, as we sat talking to David's son, David slipped away and we heard the sound of a trumpet. When we went to the door we found David sitting on the front porch, playing for some of the younger people in the settlement. Outside, on the bare ground in front of the house, they were dancing a quadrille. It was the quadrille as it had been danced a hundred years before, and they were laughing as they danced, whirling and turning in the darkness. When he finished playing and the dancers straggled back toward their own houses, David told us that he 'began studying how to play the trumpet' when he was 49 years old, and that he expected that if he kept studying he would get better. He was determined to play as well as a friend from a neighboring settlement who was also a trumpet player.

After we'd come back into the house and we were sitting down in the living room again there was a new interruption. A short, spindly, edgy man in even more ragged clothes than the other men we'd seen on Andros wore, stood uncomfortably inside the door. His skin was dark and it was difficult to see his face in the faint yellow gleam of the kerosene lamp. He had heard that we were looking for a sloop to take us across the bights to Mangrove Cay. With David doing most of the talking we settled on a price and after a moment he slipped away. He would take us in the morning.

We had come close now, but what did David know about McQueen? David shook his head. He couldn't say much about him. He hadn't heard Frederick sing in years, and he knew that he was drinking too much rum, but like Captain Ormond Johnson, who had also told me about the night singing, he could never forget hearing Frederick sing in the sponging days, when on calm nights the boats would tie up so close that the men could walk across the decks from one to another, and the singing would go on until morning. We sat

up with David into the night, while he told us the legends of
the animals and spirits of Andros.

At dawn David and his son carried our things down to the
pier, we shook hands goodbye, and one of the men from the
settlement sculled us out to the small sloop that was taking
us to Mangrove Cay. It was an older boat, the sails in shreds,
the lines spliced from a dozen partings, the hull thick with
weathered paint that had worn to no distinguishable color.
The sloop was about thirty feet long, and it wallowed sluggishly at the end of its anchor ropes, its well filled with sea
water. The deck was bare and the boards had dried out in the
years of burning sunlight and begun to separate. There was a
small cabin, but it was stuffed with old sails and fishing gear.
There was no motor. The only crew were the man who had
come to David Mackey's house and a teenage boy who watched
us uncomfortably, not sure what he should say if we spoke to
him.

Neither Ann nor I had ever been sailing before the summer
on Andros. We didn't grow up around people who owned sail
boats. After we came back we were often asked what we
thought of sailing in the Bahamas, and when would we go out
on a sailboat again. Neither of us has been on a sailboat since
that summer. The day on the sloop that took us from Behring
Point ended any excitement we had ever felt at the idea of
depending on the wind to take any kind of journey.

There was almost no wind when the sloop's captain pulled
in the frayed lines and we moved slowly out of the shelter of
the shallow anchorage. The sails flapped listlessly, but there
was enough tide to drift us across the wide mouth of the
North Bight toward an island called Big Wood Cay. When
we had come to about thirty yards from the beach of Big
Wood the last breath of wind died and we lay becalmed. The
settlement we had left, Behring Point, shimmered in the heat

behind us. Beyond the line of reef a sloop from the south of the island lay as still as we did. Voices occasionally reached us across the water. The hours passed. On the small sloop there was no place to hide from the sun, or from the small flies with a nasty sting that had found the boat as they buzzed out to us from the island. There was a little water on board, but it was in a rusted oil can, almost unfit to drink.

About noon a light breeze slowly carried us past the island. Despite our discomfort it was beautiful around the boat's drifting wake. We were sailing over the warm shallows of a coral reef, and below us were the myriad, dazzling colors of fish and sea plants. Ann knelt against the railing, the sun-light and the flies momentarily forgotten as she leaned over the shining water, one hand holding her straw hat, staring down into the gleaming current.

We still had just begun to learn that the mood of the sea, in a moment, can turn sullen and dangerous, even with the sky clear and the sun sparkling on the crests of the swells. We had been drifting too long, and the changing tide was carrying us out toward the reef. Our slow progress had taken us out into the current of the Middle Bight. The Middle Bight is nearly a mile across, and a heavy current surges through it with the tides. The boatmen suddenly stood up and stared at the line of surf that was creeping steadily toward us. If the boat crashed into it, even at our slow, drifting speed, the weight of the water in the well would probably stove in one side of the worn hull. We would break up in forty feet of water, too far from the beach for any of our things or our tapes or the tape recorder to be saved, and we would have to swim back to the island and wait until someone could pick us up.

The ragged man who owned the boat was as badly prepared for an accident as he was with drinking water or food. There was a weathered oar lying against one of the railings and the boy trailed it over the stern of the boat and began trying to scull us across the streaming current. There were two long poles lying on the deck. The captain picked up one of them and I picked up the other and we began trying to pole the boat along, bending over the railing, searching in the water for any rock or growth of coral to push against. The three of us might as well have been trying to stop the wind by holding up our arms. The boat was so waterlogged that nothing we did slowed its drift. The reef was only fifty yards from us and we could hear the water breaking over it.

But we had also just begun to learn that it is impossible to predict what the sea will do next. As the four of us stood on the deck, our eyes shaded against the blaze of the sun on the water there was a flurry of spray on the cresting swells. Suddenly a summer squall came up. We could feel a hot wind against our skin. The sails flapped and filled. Slowly the boat came around, and we dropped our poles and the oar on the deck. The captain of the boat looked at us and nodded gravely, his expression studied, as if he'd known from the beginning what would happen. In a few moments the reef and the flies were behind us and we sailed through the surging current from the last of the bights, with only a few miles still to go to Mangrove Cay.

We dropped anchor a few hundred yards from a beautiful, palm-lined beach. There were dinghies pulled up on the sand and a few houses, but there were very few people to be seen. Most of the settlement seemed to be out on the boats or back in the bush tending their gardens. The water between us and the shore was a pale green. It was shallow, and even if the sloop could have come in closer to the beach there was no pier of any kind. We transferred our bags and the recording equipment into a tiny, leaking skiff and sculled toward the shore, bailing as we went. Twenty yards from the beach the skiff grounded in the soft sand. I had to jump off the side and wade

ashore, holding the tape recorder above my head to keep it out of the waist-deep water. I have never forgotten the feeling of the warm sea and the soft sand under my feet as I clambered away from the skiff.

The wind that had taken us away from the reef had stiffened, and the lowering clouds had turned the afternoon into a dark passage of flailing trees and scattering dead leaves on the path in front of us. We were hurrying toward a combination dance hall and grocery store that had electricity and rooms. The rain began to crash against the hanging palm fronds above us and we walked as hurriedly as we could, stopping to catch our breath in the small stone buildings beside the path that sold cheap rum. We finally stumbled into the dance hall soaking wet, badly sunburned, and still shaking from our experience on the drifting sloop.

The dance hall had food, and after we had slept for an hour and washed and eaten another supper of Andros chicken, we began asking about McQueen. A man at the bar in the dance hall who was from Bastian Point, three miles from the settlement where McQueen was staying, said that McQueen's boat, *The Charity*, was still at sea, but that it was expected in at any time. The next morning the owner of the dance hall, a trim, energetic man named Prince Albert Jolly, let us borrow bicycles and we rode toward McQueen's settlement at Lisbon Creek. The stony, bone-shaking path ended at Bastian Point, and we pushed the bicycles across the heavy sand toward the creek. When we passed a grove of coconut palms we saw a man constructing the frame of a native dinghy and we stopped to catch our breath. He was trimming the mahogany ribs on a rough work bench set up under the trees. A man who was from Lisbon Creek was sitting on a log talking with him. When we asked about McQueen they both laughed. The man from Lisbon Creek shook his head.

'All he lives for is drinking.'

'Does he still sing?'

'Sometimes. But when he gets drinking he doesn't sing so good.'

The man stood up and said he would walk with us to his settlement. He was a tall, slim, broad-shouldered man, with a strongly molded face and jaw and a direct, serious expression. His skin was dark. His hair was trimmed short. His name was Leroy Bannister — Captain Leroy Bannister. Over the next few days he and his wife took us into their house and into the life of their settlement as we waited for *The Charity*.

Captain Bannister was a hard-working, and — by Andros standards — a very prosperous man. His dinghy had come in first in the Bahamian work boat races the winter before, and his smaller sloop had taken second. He had a large sloop for crawfishing and an extensive farm not far from the settlement. He seemed happy, but as we learned in our long talks together he and his wife, several years before, had lost their two young children in a fire, and they had no other children. He was the only man of his family still living, and the name of Bannister in his part of Andros would die with him. He felt very keenly the pain of not having someone to leave his name to. His wife was a very attractive woman who wore neatly-sewn dresses and covered her head with a small sun hat. She worked from dawn until ten or eleven at night on the endless jobs that had to be done by the women in the settlements.

Under the trees at Lisbon Creek there were six large sloops under construction. The building methods looked primitive. A rough frame was built on the sand, and the wooden pieces of the ribs and hull and planking were cut and trimmed with hand-held saws and drills, then pegged into place on the keel. The half-finished skeleton of ribs and planks looked like a large insect rising out of the sand. The Lisbon Creek men were known for their skills at constructing fast, strong boats, and they often found themselves with more orders than they could handle. They were scattered along the beach, working on all of the boats at the same time, their shirts off, their backs gleaming with perspiration. There was a low-throttled

sound of gasoline-driven electric generators set up on the
sand beside the piled lumber, and a whir of electric saws and
drills. I was relieved to see the generators. The tape recorder
had to have a power source to operate, and I could see that the
houses, like those at Behring Point, were without electricity.

A handsome young woman in a loose dress and a scarf
draped under her hat walked toward us along the beach and
Captain Bannister called out to her. Her husband, Richard
Bastian, was the captain of *The Charity* and McQueen stayed
in a room in their house. She was waiting for the first glimpse
of the sail, but with the fitful winds she didn't know when
The Charity might come in. We walked with Bannister to his
house and we sat in his neatly furnished living-room for the
rest of the afternoon while he told us about his boats and
about the people of the settlement. He called to his wife, who
was cleaning fish in the kitchen, and asked her if she would
mind if we stayed until *The Charity* came in. No, her voice
came back from the kitchen. No, she wouldn't mind, and she
came into the room nodding and smiling to show us that she
meant it. He stood up and said he would make the arrange-
ments to have our things brought from the dance hall where
we had left them on Monday morning. His dinghy would
come for everything so we wouldn't have to carry the bags and
the equipment seven miles on the rough path.

Ann wanted to walk before we sat down to eat and she took
her camera down to the creek. The men in the settlement
worked on their own boats at the same time they were building new sloops further along the shore. Their sloops were
pulled up into the shallow water, and the ebbing tide left
them canted on their sides, their masts criss-crossing in hap-
hazard patterns. She became so intrigued by the patterns of
the masts and the painted names on the sterns of the boats
that she took off her shoes and waded out into the water to

take a photograph. The clouds had cleared away again and there was a softened, late afternoon light washing over the weathered hulls and the tangled lines hanging from the tilted masts. The picture became the cover of the first of the albums to be released of our recordings a few months later.

Dinner was rice and fish, and the fish was scored and flavored with pepper. We were so used to the taste now that it was hard to remember that fish had ever tasted any other way.

12

The Day Is So Long and the Wages So Small

There was nothing we could do about the sloop that was somewhere out on the sea, waiting for the winds and the tides. The hours we had spent drifting helplessly across the Middle Bight in our becalmed sloop had left us with a cautious respect for the forces of the wind and the currents that the men struggled against in their boats. Everyone else in the settlement was so used to the uncertainty that life went on around us without any sign of concern or interruption. The only indication that anyone was waiting was the sight of Captain Bastian's wife as she walked up and down the beach, sometimes with her hands clasped in front of her, supporting the weight of her coming baby.

Prince Albert Jolly, who owned the dancehall and store where we had stayed when we had first come to Mangrove Cay, sent word for the local brass band to come play for us and they arrived about nine o'clock with their drums and trumpets. The drum was another wooden keg covered with goat skin, and we had to wait until the heat from a small fire had tightened the head enough for the band to play. The men in the band had come in their ordinary work clothes, barefoot, and wearing battered hats to keep off the sun. Jolly had a gasoline generator behind his store, so there was electricity. I had no problems setting up the tape recorder, and the men sat on the long benches or on the worn wooden chairs inside the dancehall, tuning up their instruments.

It was an ordinary morning of music, in the outdoors, with the palm trees stretching up into the sunlight around us. But like all the other music we heard that summer what they played was layered with so many complex influences. The band, named 'The Daniel Saunders Brass Band', had only three members; Daniel Saunders and Erskine Green, who played the trumpets, and Edgar Green, who played the drum. They were young and earnest, and they began with a hymn, 'In The Sweet Bye And Bye'. They played it the same way the brass band we'd recorded in Fresh Creek had played their hymns — simple and sincere and with a heavy thumping beat that was as four-square as a wooden box. They played with serious expressions, trying not to puff out their cheeks, treating each simple harmony as if it were a precious stone. It was a fitting expression of the culture that the British colonialists had left for them.

Then just as they finished the hymn another musician, as young as they were, with a mandolin hanging on a string around his neck, came racing along the beach on a bicycle. We had already gathered a crowd with the drum beats and the tuning of the two trumpets, and as soon as they saw him coming the people began to jump with excitement. His name was Harold Finley, and everyone knew about him and his mandolin playing. When Finley hurriedly tuned his instrument and joined in, the music abruptly changed. Suddenly the rhythm took on the loose elasticity of all the island's other musical styles that had lingering traces of an African past. The trumpets still started each piece playing in harmony, as if they were consciously trying to fuse their two musical cultures, but already the drum and the mandolin were creating a more complicated beat beneath them. The brassy sound flared out over the heads of the men and women crowded into the small dancehall. The two trumpet players, once past the opening harmonies, tried to outdo each other as the women

leaped and danced around them. Finley's mandolin was strung with plastic ukelele strings so the tone of his instrument was very soft, but his fine rhythm and the abruptly exuberant drumming had completely altered the band's sound. It had become almost like a small jazz band. Each of the trumpet players tried to create real solos, despite the obvious fact that neither of them spent much time practising. They played all the types of old style dance music — polkas and quadrilles, and there was even a guileless version of the old children's song in waltz tempo, 'My Bonnie Lies Over The Ocean'.

We had only asked them to play a few pieces, and we could hear that the two trumpet players were going to run down before they played much longer. Finley and the drummer could have played for the rest of the morning, but we also wanted to get our things ready so we could move them to Lisbon Creek. The musicians listened back to what they'd played, hitting each other on the back and singing along, then the trumpets went back in their cases, Finley strung his mandolin around his neck and picked up his bicycle, and the crowd dispersed noisily back into the settlement.

We left everything at the dancehall, under Prince Jolly's eyes, and took our bicycles back along the stony path toward Lisbon Creek. As we were starting south along the ocean a man hailed us and said there was a sail coming in on the other side of the reef. It looked like *The Charity*, standing well off the reef, beating past Mangrove Cay toward Lisbon Creek. We reached the settlement just as *The Charity* dropped anchor, about five hundred yards out. People from the settlement began straggling down to the beach. Leroy Bannister saw us standing in the water, looking toward the sloop, and called out.

'Do you want to go out to her?'

We did. Bannister hoisted the sail on a dinghy tied near

his house and we went out to *The Charity*. There were some children on the deck, coming back from a trip to Nassau, and they were helping Captain Bastian load supplies into a skiff. As we shouted to the boat across the water Frederick McQueen climbed out of the cabin on to the deck. He was tall, over six feet, very dark-skinned. His chest was tremendous, but his arms and legs looked thin, almost wasted. When I climbed on to the deck he shook hands nervously, answering my questions in a light, clear voice. We unloaded the sloop and sailed in to the settlement. Bannister had to sail back to Mangrove Cay for the equipment we'd left there after we'd recorded the brass band only a few hours earlier, and I left with him, in the dinghy again, almost immediately.

It was after dark when we finally made our way back to Lisbon Creek with the tape recorder and our bags. I was almost too excited to eat, but Captain Bannister's wife had cooked supper and we ate quickly. We had found McQueen, but we still hadn't heard him sing. Mrs Bannister came in from the kitchen and said that she had heard from Captain Bastian's wife that there had been a wake while the boats were in Nassau. The sloops had tied up side by side away from the public dock, and there had been singing all night, with prizes for the best lead singer. How had McQueen done? He had won, just as he always did. The rest of the crew had all but carried him back to *The Charity* with the bright colored scarves that were given out as the prizes draped around his neck. Bannister said that McQueen had only come close to losing once that anybody knew about. He was singing in a contest with one of the Bullards, a famous family of singers from Long Bay Cays, but he had realized that it was going to be a close contest, so he didn't drink anything and his voice held up all through the night. I went out into the darkness, looking for McQueen, feeling reassured.

Most of the people from the settlement were sitting on a small concrete pier talking quietly, or just sitting and enjoying the evening breeze. Except for the murmuring voices and a low buzz of insects the night was completely still. I asked where McQueen had gone, and he answered me from the darkness a few yards away. I walked over to talk to him. After a moment he said,

'Everybody say I shouldn't let you down. Don't worry, I won't let you down.'

I was too embarrassed to answer him.

About twenty minutes later we heard shouting from the other side of the settlement. There was a sound of guitar music. Some of the young men from a nearby settlement had come to hear themselves on tape. They were playing as they came, with friends behind them carrying lanterns. We knew one of them. It was Prince Forbes, who had been on the sloop that drifted into Fresh Creek for the August Monday weekend, and who had played in H. Brown's pick-up dance band beside the creek. The tape machine was set up on the porch of Bannister's house, and Bannister and I went with three or four other men to trace our primitive extension cords back to one of their gasoline-driven electric generators. The men had enclosed it in an earth oven that the women used for cooking outside their houses, hoping that the thick walls would muffle some of the sound. The cords I had brought were only household equipment, but if no one tripped over the lines in the darkness and pulled the plugs apart the system would work well enough for us to record. When we came back to the house, walking with Bannister's flashlight, I noticed that McQueen was gone.

The young men with their guitars had also brought a bottle of rum and most of the people from the settlement had crowded around by the time they finished playing. Forbes knew about the recordings we had done with Spence, but he only laughed and said he played the same way so he knew we would like to hear him. He usually played for church groups and he spent most Sunday mornings sitting on the beach at his own settlement playing hymns. He was considered to be the best guitarist on the south of the island, and the recording turned into a small party before he'd finished. He did play with a little of Spence's individual technique, but there was none of Spence's inventiveness or excitement. When he listened back Forbes grinned wryly. The other guitarists were showing off to their friends and there were roars of laughter at the sound of the instruments over the machine.

About midnight I saw McQueen standing at the edge of the crowd and I called to him, asking him if he was ready to sing. He nodded. I asked him if he would stand out in the yard and lead the people of the settlement in a boat launching song. He stood in the open space, the golden light from the lanterns on the porch casting deep shadows across the trampled clearing. The people spread in a self-conscious, ragged circle against the darkness of the trees around him. There was a nervous silence; then he put his hand against his ear to steady the tone of his voice, lifted his head and began to sing. His voice was clear and brilliant, with a tender sadness. We had never heard the song before.

The day is so long and the wages so small.

With uncertain voices a few of the people in the circle joined him singing the chorus line, when they would all pull on the ropes to draw one of the newly built sloops off the beach into water. They sang:

Long summer day.

The first line was repeated:

The day is so long and the wages so small.

Now McQueen joined the other voices for the chorus line that ended the verse.

> She's a long summer day.

As his voice carried into the shadows the darkness inside him seemed to lift. The others fell silent and stepped back to listen to him.

> I say Captain you gae launch this boat now today.
>   Long summer day.
> I say who knows the captain of the boat now this
> morning,
>   Long summer day.

> Captain Leroy you now going to launch now your boat,
>   Long summer day.
> I say everybody now is happy on the Creek now,
>   Long summer day.

> Yeah, the day is so long and the wages so small,
>   Long summer day.
> Oh boys I say take it now easy, the crawfish is comin' on,
>   Long summer day.

> I say take now easy boys, 'cause the crawfish they're
> come now,
>   Long summer day.
> Oh Lord the day is so long and the wages so small,
>   Long summer day.

In the stillness, when he stopped singing, I realized I was crying.

13

McQueen

Once McQueen had finished leading the launching song, the mood changed. The people who knew him in the settlement realized that he wasn't drunk and that he wanted to sing for us. There was a stir of laughter at the edges of the yard. Shadows moved as people began to edge a little nearer to us. I wanted him to come on the porch and sing, so I could get closer with the microphone. I also wanted some of the men to come up on the porch with him and sing the bass harmonies. McQueen was smiling and nodding, turning to look around at the faces of his neighbors. There was almost a child-like expression to his face, and moods and uncertainties shifted across it like the clouds reflected on the surface of the sea. He was wearing a short-sleeved shirt with the sleeves rolled up two or three turns, his thin arms oddly fitting with his rangy shoulders and his powerful chest.

Despite their obvious embarrassment two of the men came up the steps and stood a little way from him. When he began to sing again, first one, then the other, leaned closer to add their voices in an improvised harmony to the last line of the verse. The song was the ballad 'Cecil Gone In The Time Of Storm', the finest of the Andros ballads. We had already heard it in Fresh Creek when John Roberts sang it for us, but McQueen's performance took the song's story into dimensions we had only sensed before. He was standing against the stucco wall of the porch of the Bannister's house, his head thrown back, perspiring with the intensity of the singing. In the shadows, beyond the yellow glare of the lanterns, other voices hummed and sang the last line, 'Cecil gone in the time of storm'.

Now in nineteen hundred and thirty-three,
On a blessed Sunday day, praise the Lord,
Some souls was crossing Jordan's River stream,
    Cecil gone in the time of storm.

Tell you nineteen hundred and thirty-three,
On that blessed Sunday day, oh Lord,
Some souls was crossing Jordan's River's stream.
    Cecil gone in the time of storm.

I remember that boy and his mother had a talk,
He decide to go to Mastic Point.
Take his suitcase in his hand, walking down along the bay,
    Cecil gone in the time of storm.

Lord, he get into the boat, yes he hoist the boat sail you know,
Start to go to Mastic Point.
When the boat get confound, poor Cecil get drowned,
    Cecil gone, oh yes, Cecil gone.

I remember the time passed, for eight days time,
The boy weren't turned back home any more.
When they make up in their mind to go to Blanket Sound land,
    Cecil gone, oh yes, Cecil gone.

When they reach to Blanket Sound they met his uncle on the beach,
Say, 'You ain't seen Cecil nowhere?'

'I believe Cecil reach all the way to Nicholas Town.'
    Cecil gone, oh yes, Cecil gone.

I remember these questions what my friend now did
say,
I believe Cecil now get drowned.
Oh blessed Lord, that my dearest friend is gone,
    Cecil gone in the time of storm.

When they a week now around, bound to Blanket
Sound land,
They met now his mother on the bay.
This is the question what Eudie now did ask,
    Cecil gone in the time of storm.

'I find the boat, I find the sail,
None of his body I behold?'
I said, 'Oh, now my cousin, I believe Cecil drowned.'
    Cecil gone in the time of storm.

I remember now that woman now, she fell on the bay,
She rolled all over the bay.
Say, 'I didn't know God would no answer my cry'
    Cecil gone in the time of storm.

I remember that woman, Lord, she fell on the bay,
She rolled all over the bay.
Say, 'Oh, blessed Lord, there my youngest son was
gone.'
    Cecil gone in the time of storm.

These the last words I remember what the woman did
say,
'Oh God, make peace with his soul.
If a man live in Christ, you sure will die right.'
    Cecil gone, oh yes, and he's gone.

McQueen's voice was a strong, high tenor, and the song was high even for him. There was a moment of strain on the highest note of the first verse, but after that his voice opened to the tones, and words at the ends of the phrases rang with a throbbing vibrato. At the end of each verse he half sang, half hummed a tone that carried to the beginning of the next verse, phrasing his note to the other men's voices. As he sang I could hear why he had always won his singing contests. He didn't simply repeat the words and the melody, he interpreted the story. When he described Cecil's mother coming to look for her son, in the line, 'I find the boat, I find the sail, none of his body I behold?' his voice became delicate as a woman's and he acted out her fearful questioning as if he were Eudie himself.

The ballad, for McQueen, was also personal, in a way that it hadn't been when Roberts sang it. Roberts' performance was more detailed, but he had sung it in the third person — he was describing what he had been told about, what others had seen. John had sung:

> Oh Lord, now she said to the people, 'Oh my son,
> My son has gone now, we will see him no more,'
> Nobody knows what become of Cecil gone,
>   Cecil gone in the time of storm.

At the same point in the song McQueen sang:

> 'I find the boat, I find the sail,
> None of his body I behold?'
> I said, 'Oh, now my cousin, I believe Cecil drowned.'
>   Cecil gone in the time of storm.

Another quality of McQueen's singing that had made him so respected, despite his obvious emotional vulnerability, was his voice itself. His voice had a natural clear purity, and with his large chest he could sing with ringing power. Then as a final dimension there was the sensitivity and the expressive-

ness that made his singing unlike anything else I had ever
heard.

He sang part of another ballad, but the other men didn't
know it. There was some uncertainty about what to do next.
It was well after midnight and it felt like the moment to
finish for the night. He was going to sing for us again the
next day, and we would continue with the recording then.

People slowly scattered, most of them with flashlights that
bobbed like fireflies in the darkness. I groped along my
extension cords, pulling them out of the sand and unplug-
ging them before they were damaged by someone stepping on
them. I hadn't noticed the insects before, I hadn't heard the
sound of the sea. Everything had been going on in the shadows around us, the mosquitoes had whined out of the shadows
and the surf had surged up on the beach, but I had only heard
McQueen's voice.

There are moments in our lives that we remember more
clearly and more immediately than others, and for our months
in Andros I also had the notes that had piled up along with
the tapes in the bag I had for microphones, extension cords,
plugs, and converters. But even without the notes I still can
remember the food that Captain Bannister's wife cooked for
us. She had decided she wanted us to try all of the different
things that were to be had on Andros. For lunch, sitting in
their neat dining-room around the table with a white cro-
cheted cloth, we ate doves that had been shot in the steamy
wilderness of brush behind the garden plots. For breakfast she
had prepared fish with brown gravy. She had cooked it with
less pepper than we had become used to in Fresh Creek, and
under the thick gravy there was a pleasant taste of fish.

When we had eaten, Ann went for a walk in the settlement

with Captain Bannister's wife, and Bannister and I set up the gasoline generator and the extension cords to power the tape recorder. When we were finally set up, early in the afternoon, McQueen had already come to the house and he was sitting nervously on a wooden chair at the side of the room. I could sense that part of the wariness the other people in the settlement felt around McQueen reflected more than their disapproval of his drinking. He was also intense and moody, and I realized that he often couldn't control his moods himself. Other people had straggled in, and when they had filled all of the chairs they squatted on the floor. McQueen was ringed with expectant faces.

One of the older sloop captains from Lisbon Creek, Joseph Green, had come with McQueen to sing bass. Richard Bastian, the captain of McQueen's sloop, often added the bass harmonies when McQueen was out at sea or in Nassau, but he would only sing religious songs, and he hadn't come forward to add his voice to the launching song or the ballad the night before. Green was from another settlement, several miles away, but everyone on Andros always was able to get from one part of the island to another if they heard that something was happening. He was thin-faced and gray-haired, and he wore a dark visored cap to emphasize his status as a captain. He also was one of the few musicians left on Andros who played the old style wooden fife, and he had an extensive knowledge of Andros folk customs. He hadn't, however, sung much with McQueen, and on one of the songs he could be heard struggling to sing high enough to harmonize with McQueen's melody. In the background he complained, 'It's too sharp,' meaning too high in pitch.

The singing started with the ballad McQueen had given up the night before, 'Harcourt Got Drowned In The Luggerhead Hole'. It was another ballad about a drowning, this time in a place known as a luggerhead — the Bahamian word for turtle — hole. This ballad wasn't nearly as developed as 'Cecil Gone

In The Time Of Storm', and he soon had to begin improvising words and phrases to fill in the story. We listened to a little of the tape, then — before he could begin again — suddenly it began to rain. We were caught in a heavy downpour. The house had a corrugated iron roof, and the noise of the rain on the roof made it impossible to record. There were about twenty people jammed into the small room and we waited in the suffocating heat for the rain to stop. The drumming of the rain was so insistent that we couldn't even talk to each other.

When the rain finally blew over, McQueen's mood had changed. He had withdrawn into himself with a deep inner concentration. He began singing with an almost frightening intensity. The first song was the beautiful 'Dig My Grave', and this time Captain Bastian joined him, leaning toward the microphone from the place against the wall where he was standing. Bastian was much younger than McQueen, solidly built, with a round, dark, lined face. He was one of the few young singers on Andros who had tried to learn the old style. McQueen was hunched forward to the edge of his chair and his body was tense with concentration. His hand was against his ear and his eyes were squeezed shut. The layering of rhythm that was so important to the rhymers helped free McQueen's improvisations, and Bastian's bass melodies took on a freer beat as the songs grew and shaped themselves in the oppressive heat of the crowded room. Bastian soon was as excited as Frederick. For the rhyming spiritual 'Kneeling Down Beside The Gate' I held the microphone closer to him so that it would be possible to hear the 'bassing' style more clearly. All of us were soaked with perspiration. I could see Ann's face glistening among the bunched people seated at McQueen's feet.

It had been difficult to find someone in the settlement who was willing to sing treble with McQueen. His own voice was very high and it was so powerful that the other men were embarrassed to sing with him, but the sound of the voices in

Bannister's house was loud enough to be heard everywhere in the settlement. After a few minutes, in the middle of one of the songs, there was the sound of someone singing a treble part from outside the window. It was an older man in the settlement, Norris Rolle, who was building a boat on the beach several hundred yards away. He had been unable to stay away from the singing, and he had stopped work and come to the house. The men ended the afternoon with Norris kneeling on the floor, since every chair was taken, Bastian crouched over, his eyes closed like McQueen's and a hand against his ear to hear the tone. The last song was the hymn sometimes used to end prayer meetings, 'Shake My Hand'.

> Shake my hand and wish me goodbye,
> Oh my blessed Saviour . . .

McQueen was half singing, half chanting, his body twisting with the effort of his performance as he leaned forward and reached out to shake hands with the people staring up at him from the floor, their bodies swaying along with his, their eyes wide with their own excitement.

When McQueen finally stood up and looked around at us, his shirt wringing with perspiration, his face shining, his mouth open to catch his breath, the crowd in the room began slowly to push back the chairs and stand up from the floor. Norris Rolle picked up the hammer he had left outside the window and went back to the boat frame. I went outside with McQueen and shook his hand. I couldn't think of anything to say. We had talked about everything the night before, what I would pay him and what I wanted to do with the recordings. I handed him the last of the money we had saved to pay our singers and musicians. He nodded nervously and without glancing at it pushed it into the pocket of his sweat-soaked shirt. Then he turned and went slowly down the steps and along one of the paths toward the beach.

I still had a few moments of tape left, and the late afternoon was clear and quiet. We recorded a few more pieces with Joseph Green's small fife spilling out the old, half-forgotten dance tunes. Captain Bastian played a hymn, 'Under The Precious Blood', on the harmonica he took with him to fill some of the quiet on the sea. Ann and I looked at each other across the room and, aware of the other people in the room watching us, smiled a little self-consciously. Our search for the music of Andros was over.

Breakfast the next morning was another adventure in Bahamian food tastes. There on our plates were what looked like small white arms with hands and fingers. At our first glance it looked as though Mrs Bannister had found dolls' arms for us to try. What was on our plates was iguana, the large lizards we sometimes heard scurrying away in the brush. The usual description of something like iguana or snake is that the flesh tastes like chicken. The iguana was tender and easily chewed, so it didn't have the texture of a tough, yard-fed Bahamas chicken, but it didn't taste like chicken either. The best description Ann and I could agree on was that it tasted like we expected an iguana would taste. But without pepper the flavor was mild, almost colorless, different from the fiery fish we'd been eating.

The wooden sloops, like all wooden boats left in water, had to be regularly pulled up out of the water and scrubbed and mended and recaulked, and the boats that Ann had waded into the water to photograph had to be drawn back into the deeper water when the men were through working on the hulls. Bannister was going to the beach to help with the lines when they refloated a sloop they'd finished repairing. I asked if I could come along, and I soon found myself up to my waist in water, groping in the sand for someplace under the hull of the boat to slip a line. The sloop was heavy and waterlogged, and as I splashed around it I felt like I was beside a beached whale that would come to life if we could somehow only get it back to the sea.

When I finally straightened up, I looked over at the beach where several men were holding the other end of the line, and there, at the front, was McQueen. It was obvious that he had been drinking most of the night. There was a faint cast to his dark skin, and even from twenty yards away I could see his unfocused, reddened eyes. He was still in the clothes he'd been wearing the day before, and I was sure he'd never taken them off. His hands were trembling on the line, but he knew that he was supposed to be there at the creek working with the others, so he had joined them to pull the boat out into the creek. Another man walking along the beach towards us saw him and called out in a jeering tone, 'Frederick, what you do with your money? You spend it all?'

McQueen's expression changed. Child-like, he dropped the line and looked in his pocket for the money I had given him. His face showed his surprise. He had drunk so much that I wasn't sure he even remembered what had happened to the money.

'You find the money, Frederick?' the man jeered again.

The men holding on to the line laughed, but their laughter was low and uncomfortable. I realized that they had known Frederick all their lives, and under the roughness of their banter around him there was pity and a kind of love. He fumbled for the line again, and with a hard, grinding drag at the lines we began the struggle to return our clumsy, unwilling, stranded boat to its element.

14

Last Long Summer Days

After all our struggles getting to Andros it was disconcert-
ingly simple to get off of the island. We had another day at
Lisbon Creek with Leroy Bannister and his wife. They put on
their best clothes and posed for Ann's camera in front of their
house. Then they changed back into their everyday clothes
and we walked along the beach, calling out to the men back
at work at their boat building. We climbed into the dinghy
Leroy had pulled up close to the shore, we looked at a small
sloop he had built the year before and was trying to sell. We
were told that McQueen had gone with Captain Bastian to
pick up some supplies and they wouldn't be back until the
next afternoon. It was an ordinary Andros day.

The next morning the mail boat anchored off of Mangrove
Cay, and this time, in calm, sunny weather, we had no problems taking the equipment and our luggage in a small boat
off the pier. The ship was crowded for this trip, but we found
space on a bench and stayed in the cabin out of a rain squall
until we anchored in Nassau. After the calm of Andros Nassau was a frantic buzz of activity, but when we left Bay Street
behind us again and found our way through the dirt streets to
the worn wooden gate of the guest house where we had stayed
at the beginning of the summer the small city seemed to lapse
again into its mood of quiet calm. The owner of the guest
house, his dark face as expressionless as we remembered,
pushed open the gate and he allowed himself a brief half smile

as he saw who we were. The room above the bar that we had rented before was empty, we could stay there again if we wanted. We took the bags back up the narrow stairs, this time without the struggle we'd gone through months before. Whatever else had happened to us on Andros we had come back wirier and a little stronger.

In the evening we ate again at one of the bare tables in the bar-room. Fish and rice, but with only a hint of pepper, and the beer was colder. The only other people in the bar-room were men the owner obviously had known for many years. Wondering what they would say about the music we had traveled to Andros to find we brought the tape recorder back downstairs, set it up on a table, and played some of the songs from Fresh Creek. The owner, again in one of his white shirts and dark trousers, listened and nodded his head.

'That's the old way. That's the old way when I grew up.'

It seemed to be completely natural to him that some of the people on Andros were still singing like that. What was still a little confusing to all of them was that Ann and I were so excited by it. He didn't seem to be concerned about any of the music as part of a tradition that he shared with the Andros people. One of the men called out from another table.

'Those boys a little behind.'

The owner smiled indulgently. 'They know how to do it. We have to give them that. They know how to do it.'

'When I go back to my settlement all the boys they sing like that.'

'No,' the owner turned to look back at the table. 'These boys know. They can do it.'

When it was darker, and cooler, we walked back to Bay Street. Since it was the end of the summer the stream of tourists had thinned down, but there was still the jangle of pizza parlors and fish restaurants and bars, and the crowds of restless boys along the sidewalks waiting for something to happen. Across the water we could see the lights of Paradise Island, with its Miami Beach-style hotels and its gaudy tourist attractions. We knew that we would never see Andros again the way it had been that summer — so isolated in its own time and its own century — but what would it finally be like there, when there were more hotels like the one we had seen struggling at Fresh Creek? When more Americans had bought up the best land along the beaches and harbors, when there was more electricity, and with it radio and television? Was this what was waiting for the people we had known there? I thought about the children of the families we had seen working their small, stony gardens and sailing their hand-built sloops, gathering shells, and tending dark shops by kerosene lamps. Would the children spend their lives as waiters and chamber-maids and yardboys?

But even as I thought this to myself I understood that I was romanticizing the poverty of the island. I was pretending that the Andros people would rather work endless hours scratch-ing at the poor soil and bringing meager catches of fish in to Nassau in the wells of their lumbering boats than be paid a regular salary for doing work that went on for months at a time and didn't scar their hands or strain their bodies. I was valuing an isolation that the people there found stifling and defeating, and it was an isolation that Ann and I could leave simply by taking the mail boat. It was the Andros people themselves who would decide what would come next.

We were both quiet as we walked back to the guest house. For once we didn't have much to say. We had gone to the island to preserve the music that we knew would soon be lost, and it would have been enough for us to have done that much. We couldn't have foreseen that there would be Joseph Spence and John Roberts and Frederick McQueen. With their music we had found more than a tradition and a past. We had found artists who were still transforming their tradition, who were shaping it again for themselves and their communities. We had come to Andros when the traditions were still alive; when they still had meaning to the people living in the scattered settlements. That moment in a folk culture is so quickly passed, and what is left is a museum of sounds and expressions that are often beautiful, but they are as frozen in their beauty and their uniqueness as the objects in a museum's glass cases. We had come before that moment had passed, and we knew that even if our few hours of recordings wouldn't change what would happen to the island we had preserved some moments of special beauty for what would become the museum of their music. We had also, with the recordings, preserved another strand in the vital weave of music and culture that has grown out of the scattering of African peoples — people like the gentle families who had been left scattered along the beaches of Andros. We couldn't have asked for anything more than we had found.

What was also clear was that the months on Andros had changed us, even though we didn't know in what ways we would be different from what we had been when the plane landed us on the scraggly airstrip. We were still as certain that we would be together, whatever happened, even if Ann in a few weeks would be living in a dormitory room in the International House at Columbia — and I had no idea where I would be or what I would be doing. It was the kind of summer where it wasn't necessary to think of anything that might happen more than a few days away.

What we also realized, when we finally turned the last corner to our guest house, was that part of our silence was that we were tired. We were so very tired. This time we climbed slowly and stiffly up the narrow steps to our stuffy room, and in a moment we were asleep.

The cruise ship that took us back to Miami was just like the one we had taken to come to the islands, but we knew what to expect when we stopped in one of the tour offices along Bay Street and made the reservation to sail back. The people in their party clothes who had been placed at the table in the dining room with us were just as awkward and just as uncertain about what to say to us as the people had been on the journey over. Our clothes had faded in the sun and my shirt and Ann's blouse were still as obviously unironed, and neither of us had done much more than roughly cut each other's hair for the weeks we'd been on the island. They recognized, however, that we had had an experience in the Bahamas that they had missed. We were lean and tanned and my hair was sun bleached and we obviously didn't care about the cruise or the night club entertainment or the cocktail dancing that would follow it. They only nodded uncomfortably when we finished eating and left the dining-room without waiting for the cruise's evening to begin.

The upper deck was as empty as it had been when we'd sat out in the moonlight on our way to Nassau. We pulled chairs together beside the railing and we leaned back and stared up into the dark sky. The air was warm and in the steady breeze we could catch faint smells that we knew came from the island — the sunburnt earth, the scraggly plants, the streaming water at the island's shrouded center.

We didn't talk. Instead we sang. We had learned some of the songs from our tapes. I wouldn't try to rhyme, but I could sing a bass harmony to Ann's melody. We held hands and the night passed as we sat in the chairs singing.

> Oh, 'pend on me, I will 'pend on you,
> Faithful servant, I want to be;
> When you hear my trumpet sound then
> But you can depend on me . . .
>
> Now you dig my grave with a silver spade,
> But lower me down with a golden chain;

But when I hear my Father call
Then you can depend on me.

The soft air stirred around us and the sea's white churning wake widened behind us as the ship slipped through the darkness.

Miami was even hotter than we remembered. The buildings glared in the light as the ship eased into the harbor. When we collected our luggage and we stood in the crowds beside the ship, trying to find some way to get into the center of the city, it felt like the streets and the buildings had enclosed the air and then heated it up again. When we had to walk out in the blaze of the sun we felt like we were being stripped by merciless fingers. We were defenseless against the glare. We found the shabby rooming-house where we had stayed before, and left our bags and the equipment on the porch and walked around to the back of the house. The innocence of that long summer had lasted through all of our journey. Ann's car was still parked under the tree where we had left it.

APPENDIX

A check-list of the Andros Recordings, recorded by Samuel
Charters and A.R. Danberg, July and August, 1958.

Fresh Creek

Joseph Spence, guitar
Coming In On A Wing And A Prayer
The Lord Is My Shepherd
There Will Be A Happy Meeting In Glory
Glory Glory
I'm Going To Live That Life
Face To Face That I Shall Know Him
Jump In The Line
Brownskin Gal
Bimini Gal

*John Roberts, lead singer, with H. Brown, bass, and Charles
Wallace, treble*
Dig My Grave Both Long And Narrow
Depend On Me
Take Your Burden To The Lord And Leave It There
Out On The Rolling Sea
Cecil Gone In The Time Of Storm
Pytoria

John Roberts, solo
Young Gal, Swing Your Tail

The St Bartholemew's Friendly Society brass band
Kingston Brown, first trumpet; Nathaniel Mackey, second trum-
pet; Willis Thompson, snare drum; Arthur Brown, bass drum
If I Want Him To Receive Me
Kindly Light
Oh, Jesus, I Was Promised

The Fresh Creek Dance Band
H. Brown, vocal lead and maracas; Prince Forbes, guitar; Alfred
Gay, drum; James Clair, saw; local children, sticks
Mama, Bake A Johnny Cake, Christmas Coming
Gal, You Want To Go Back To Scambo
Everything The Monkey Do

Mangrove Cay

The Daniel Saunders Brass Band
Daniel Saunders, first trumpet; Erskine Green, second trumpet;
Theopolus Williams, drum
In The Sweet Bye And Bye
with Harold Finley, mandolin
Orange Blossoms Smell So Sweet — Polka
My Bonnie Lies Over The Ocean
When A Man Marries His Troubles Just Begin — Quadrille

Lisbon Creek

Frederick McQueen, singing with people of the settlement, or
with Joseph Green and Richard Bastian, bass voices, and Norris
Rolle, treble
Long Summer Days
Cecil Gone In The Time Of Storm
Harcourt Got Drowned
Dig My Grave
Curry Camp Burned Down
Jesus Will Be Your Friend
A Great Day Is Coming
Kneeling Down Beside The Gate
Shake My Hand

Prince Forbes, guitar
Take The Name Of Jesus With You
Tis So Sweet To Trust In Jesus
with Willie Green, guitar
Liza Simeon

Joseph Green, fife
I Drink All The Wine And Never Get Drunk
Bad Woman
Charles Bastian, harmonica
Under The Precious Blood

Over a period of a year and a half after our return from Andros, the recordings we had done were released by Folkways Records in New York City. Cassette copies of the four original LP releases on Folkways Records, *Music of the Bahamas*, Volume 1, Joseph Spence (FS 3844), Volume 2, John Roberts and Frederick McQueen, (FS 3845), Volume 3, Instrumental Music (FS 3846), and Joseph Spence, John Roberts and Frederick McQueen (FS 3847), can be ordered from Smithsonian Folkways Records, 955 L'Enfant Plaza SW, Suite 2600, Washington, DC 20560, USA.

Smithsonian Folkways Records has issued a CD of the nine guitar solos by Joseph Spence, and will be issuing a single CD selection of music described in this book, titled *The Day Is So Long And The Wages So Small*.